Debt Free Living

Learn How to Pay off Debt, Stay Debt Free Forever and Save Money Fast!!!

By Dermot Farrell

© 2017 and beyond Dermot Farrell

All Rights Reserved. No part of this publication may be reproduced in any form or by any means, including scanning, photocopying, or otherwise without prior written permission of the copyright holder.

Disclaimer and Terms of Use: The Author and Publisher has strived to be as accurate and complete as possible in the creation of this book, notwithstanding the fact that he does not warrant or represent at any time that the contents within are accurate due to the rapidly changing nature of the Internet. While all attempts have been made to verify information provided in this publication, the Author and Publisher assumes no responsibility for errors, omissions, or contrary interpretation of the subject matter herein. Any perceived slights of specific persons, peoples, or organizations are unintentional. In practical advice books, like anything else in life, there are no guarantees of income made. This book is not intended for use as a source of legal, business, accounting or financial advice. All readers are advised to seek services of competent professionals in legal, business, accounting, and finance field.

First Printing, 2017

Printed in the United States of America

Nothing is set in stone.

Neither poverty, wealth, or anything else.

Our past has created our present, and

Our present is creating our future,

Begin today as you mean to go on!

Table of Contents

CHAPTER ONE - YOU ARE NOT ALONE — 8

THE PROBLEM WITH CREDIT CARD DEBT	10
ALL DEBTS ARE NOT BAD DEBTS!	11
SO, WHY ARE CREDIT CARD DEBTS SO MUCH MORE DETRIMENTAL THAN OTHER DEBTS?	12
SO WHY DO SO MANY PEOPLE GET HOOKED ON CREDIT CARD DEBT?	13
SO WHAT HAS THIS EASY ACCESS TO FINANCE GOT TO DO WITH CREDIT CARDS?	15
HOW DO YOU GET YOURSELF FREE OF THE ENSNARING EFFECTS OF CREDIT CARD DEBT?	17
THE FIVE KEYS TO DEBT FREEDOM	18
FROM DEBT CYCLE TO WEALTH CYCLE	19
HOW MY WEAK FINANCIAL VALUES HAVE COST BOTH MYSELF AND MY FAMILY A GREAT DEAL!	19
IF YOU ARE NOT IN THE DRIVING SEAT, SOMEONE ELSE IS DOING THE DRIVING FOR YOU!	22
WHY IT'S NOT ENOUGH ANYMORE TO PAY OFF CREDIT CARD DEBTS	23
THE BEST WAY TO STAY OUT OF DEBT IS TO CREATE WEALTH!	27

CHAPTER TWO – THE FIRST KEY TO DEBT FREEDOM – CLEAR YOUR DEBTS — 29

THE ROLE OF INERTIA IN CREDIT CARD DEBT	35
THE ROLE OF SOCIETY AND PERSONAL FACTORS IN THE ACCRUEMENT OF NEW CREDIT CARD DEBT	38
THE FIRST KEY TO DEBT FREEDOM REDUCES DEBT AND STOPS ACCRUING NEW CREDIT CARD DEBTS & LOANS	40

CHAPTER THREE - THE SECOND KEY TO DEBT FREEDOM - BUDGETING & DEBT RELIEF PROGRAMS — 42

THE NUTS AND BOLTS OF BUDGETING AND HOW IT FITS IN WITH THE 5 KEYS OF DEBT FREEDOM	45
BUDGETING TACTICS	46
REDUCE DEBT WITH BUDGETING OR JOIN A DEBT RELIEF PROGRAM?	50
INTEGRATING BUDGETING INTO A DEBT REDUCTION PLAN	54
FINDING YOUR FINANCIAL COMPASS!	55
BUDGETING TEMPLATES	57
DO YOU KNOW WHERE YOUR LEAKS ARE?	63

CHAPTER FOUR - THE THIRD KEY TO DEBT FREEDOM - CREATE A FINANCIAL BUFFER ZONE   69

THE IMPORTANCE OF A FINANCIAL BUFFER ZONE IN THE DEBT REDUCTION PROCESS	70
HOW MUCH MONEY SHOULD I PUT INTO MY FINANCIAL BUFFER?	71
THE FINANCIAL BUFFER ZONE STRATEGY IN PRACTICE	73
SET UP A BANK ACCOUNT WHICH IS DEDICATED AS A FINANCIAL BUFFER	73
RICARDO FAMILY SAMPLE BUFFER ACCOUNT	76
MAINTAIN THE FINANCIAL BUFFER ACCOUNT EVEN AFTER YOU HAVE BECOME DEBT FREE	78
IT'S CRAZY TO CLEAR OFF DEBT, BY PAYING MINIMUM PAYMENTS ON CREDIT CARD DEBTS!	82
THE ROAD TO DEBT FREEDOM IS LITTERED WITH THE DEAD BODIES OF FINANCIALLY FAULTY IDEAS!	82

CHAPTER FIVE - THE FOURTH KEY TO DEBT FREEDOM – EFFECTIVE FINANCIAL PLANNING   84

WHY SETTING FINANCIAL GOALS IS SO NECESSARY IF YOU WANT TO REMAIN DEBT FREE!	85
HOW TO SET FINANCIAL GOALS WHICH ARE MEANINGFUL TO YOU!	88
HOW DO YOU MAKE FINANCIAL GOALS MEANINGFUL?	89
CREATING FINANCIAL GOALS DOES NOT HAVE TO BE A CHORE!	90
WHY FINANCIAL GOALS CAN BE LEISURE GOALS	93
BECOMING DEBT FREE AND REMAINING DEBT FREE BY SETTING AND FULFILLING FINANCIAL GOALS	95
INTEGRATING FINANCIAL GOAL SETTING INTO YOUR LIFE	100
NEEDS, WANTS AND DREAMS!	112
CREATING A GOAL ACHIEVEMENT TIMELINE	122
FINANCIAL PLANNING – SILLY WISH REDUCTION EXERCISE	123
REALITY CHECKING	128
THE LAW OF REALITY	128
GOAL FINDING AND PRIORITIZATION EXERCISE FLOW	122
TAKE MASSIVE ACTION!	138
CARRY OUT AN ACTION PLAN WITH THE SHORT/MEDIUM TERM GOALS	144
THE IMPORTANCE OF REVERSE ENGINEERING	146
THE NECESSITY OF REWARD SPENDING	150
SO, HOW DO YOU MONITOR SO MANY DIVERSE GOALS?	154

CHAPTER SIX - THE FIFTH KEY TO DEBT FREEDOM – CREATING WEALTH 166

GOING FROM INDEBTEDNESS TO FINANCIAL WELLBEING	167
FINANCIAL PLANNING IN PRACTICE	169
FIRST STEP IN FINANCIAL PLANNING	170
THE LAW OF ATTRACTION FALLACY!/THE REVERSE ENGINEERING FALLACY!	185
SECOND STEP IN FINANCIAL PLANNING	190
DECIDING UPON AN INVESTMENT VEHICLE WHICH FITS IN WITH YOUR FINANCIAL PLANNING	192

CHAPTER SEVEN – PUTTING THE FIVE KEYS TO OF DEBT FREEDOM TOGETHER 195

MOST IMPORTANTLY, ACTION IS VITAL!	198

Thank You   200

FOOTNOTES 201

APPENDIX 204
FREE FINANCIAL WORKSHEETS
MONTHLY EXPENDITURE WORKSHEET
FAMILY BUFFER ACCOUNT
BLUE SKY THINKING FINANCIAL PLANNING – DATE:
FINANCIAL PLANNING – SILLY WISH REDUCTION EXERCISE
PRIORITIZATION LIST
SUMMARY OF GOALS
GOAL MONITORING WORKSHEET

Illustrations

All graphs and illustrations courtesy of Tony Farrell

Chapter One - You Are Not Alone

If You Have debts You Are Not Alone!

According to data taken from The US Census, The Aggregate Revolving Consumer Debt Survey and The Survey of Consumer Finances, 160,000,000 Americans possess credit cards, which is just over half the population of America! More amazingly still, the average credit card debt of $7,219 per household in 2010! So, if you are feeling pinned down by credit card debt, you are certainly not alone!

The average indebted American is now poorer than their 1980 counterparts!

Total Inflation, from 1980 to 2010, stands at 164.6%. In 1980 the average American had $755 in revolving debt. When we add inflation to this figure we get a current value of $1,997.96. In 2010 the figure was $7,219 in revolving debt. So this debt has effectively increased by more than 250% in 30 years.

Ok, I know that statistics can be confusing, but let's just put it this way, for Americans who have managed to stay clear of debt, their disposable income is far better now than that of Americans living in the early 1980's. In general the economy has done well over the last 30 or so years, and for those who have managed to steer clear of debt, they now have substantial levels of disposable income. However, by the same token, as the figures reveal that, a great many Americans have been sucked into the credit card debt cycle!

And do remember that these are averages; many individuals have far greater levels of indebtedness than this! Ultimately, the lesson to learn from these figures is that there is no point in having a good income, if you are up to your eyeballs in debt!

And as the figures reveal, the level of indebtedness is spread out right across every strata of society. According to the 2010 Census Abstract, some 43.2% of US households hold a credit card balance. Now very nearly one in two homes in America hold credit card debt.

So to put it into perspective, if you live in an apartment block or street with 100 households, probably about 50 of them are holding credit card debt! That 43.2% figure brings the credit card debt per household figure of $7,219 up to $16,710 per indebted household

So, if you are suffering under the burden of credit card debt and are feeling isolated, well stop feeling isolated, because you are certainly not alone!

Credit Card debt has reached epidemic levels, and while for some strange reason the sheer level of credit card indebtedness is more or less overlooked by the media, the reality is staring us in the face. America, and indeed the modern developed World in general are under the vice like grip of credit card debt!

So what is it exactly that makes credit card debt so tenacious, that it has nearly half the homes in the Country in a state of indebtedness, which is thereabouts equivalent to just less than half of the yearly disposable income of the average American?

The Problem with Credit Card Debt

It's not just credit card debt which is a problem, as debts of all type and variety have taken over the lives of so many people today. Just take a look at the following graph which outlines the average level of household indebtedness in America today:

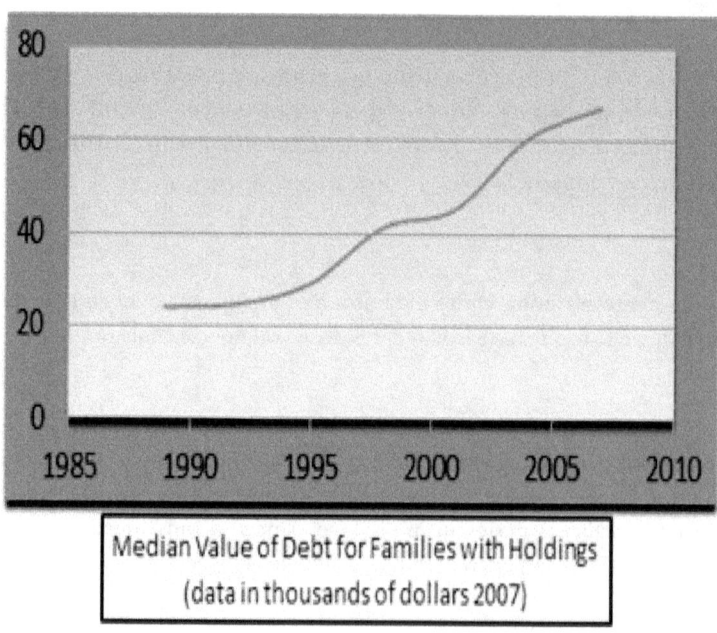

Listed in 2007 dollar figures, the average household indebtedness has increased from $24,100 in 1989 to $67,300 in 2007. That's nearly a 200% increase in household indebtedness in a period of only 18 years!

So it's not just credit card debt. Debts include the most obvious debt which is mortgage debt, which of course has increased exponentially due to the housing boom of the 1990's and early 00's. Other debts include such things as auto loans, home improvement loans, overdraft facilities, personal loans; store cards etc., the list is basically endless. Americans have taken to debt as a way of life, and as the figures suggest, many Americans are completely entrapped by their debts!

For example, a household with two incomes, which are equivalent to the 2010 average income figure of $36,697, possesses an accumulative income of $73,394. Now if this family also possesses $67,300 in debt (the 2007 average indebtedness figure), well then it doesn't take Einstein to work out that any family with this level of income to debt ratio has more than their fair share of debt!

All Debts are Not Bad Debts!

However, all debt is not bad debt. For example a home, even if it is expensive can be a good thing, especially if you like where you live. After all the debt will end at some stage and at least you will own your own home and this home will have an asset value. However, when we look at credit card debts, we see a different pattern because with credit card debt, we see high interest rates and no assets at the end of the day!

Even when we compare auto loans against credit card debt they still come out looking better, because the auto loan is set at fixed interest rates and terms, plus you get to own the car which can always be sold at some stage!

So while the general move towards ever increasing levels of indebtedness is not good, at least many loans have some redeeming features, such as an asset value for the goods purchased and fixed interest rates and loan durations. However, out of all the possible forms of debt which you can get entangled in, credit card debt is the worst kind of debt, because it has no redeeming features what so ever!

So, Why Are Credit Card Debts so Much More Detrimental Than Other Debts?

Credit cards come with the following features which manage to make credit card debt particularly intractable:

- Low monthly minimum payments

- Double digit interest rates

- Minimum payment structure which is weighted towards paying of the interest rather than the debt principal

While we will explore each of these factors in detail at a later stage, for now it is enough to know that credit card debts are designed to keep the debtor in a debt cycle, which is really difficult to get away from. For example a credit card debtor, who has say $5,000 in credit card debt, and who pays back the monthly minimum payment, will usually be paying back around 2% of the debt principal each month, which comes to $100 a month.

If the interest rate on their credit cards average out at 15% per annum, then at this rate, it will take them 7 years to clear of this debt, and that's only if they don't make any further purchases on their credit cards!

So, for many credit card debtors, they are actually paying back debts which began 5 years ago, 10 years ago or sometimes even further back! If you only make minimum payments and you keep on adding new debts on your credit cards, then it is quite possible that you are still paying back the debt principal on purchases which you made a decade ago!

Another deleterious effect of credit card debt is the utter uselessness of the majority of purchases, which are usually made on credit cards. For example if you spend money on a home loan, at least you are buying a house. Even if you buy a car, and by any means a car is a poor purchase because it devalues quickly, however it will still have some value if you decide to sell it after a couple of years.

However if you have racked up credit card debts paying your grocery bills, your holiday payments and other daily sundries, at the end of the day there is absolutely no asset value to be had in what you bought!

In a nutshell, credit card debt is an absolutely useless debt which cannot benefit you in any way at all!

So Why do so Many People

Get Hooked on Credit Card Debt?
(Debt… a drug which affects half the population of America!!!)

It's a strange reality that if half the Country were hooked on some form of drug, such as sleeping pills perhaps it would be on every newspaper in the Country, and there would be a TV documentary describing the crisis on a weekly basis. Yet strangely although half of all Americans hold credit cards, and on average they retain a balance in excess of $5,000 per year (1), it just doesn't make the headlines.

Why?

Probably because it's just so universal, practically everyone has a credit card, and while many credit card users have debt problems, most debtors who have debt problems will not mention it to anyone. Worse still many credit card users are actually credit card debtors, however they do not realize that they have a debt problem in the first place!

Put it this way, a credit card debtor may be paying out $500 a month in minimum payments, and will hardly give it a thought. However, if they decide to put a stop to their credit card debt, and they take out their various credit card bills and start to add up their balances, they may well receive a shock because at an industry average of 2% minimum payments, a minimum payment of $500 a month spells out a debt principal of $25,000!

So unless a credit card user decides to delve into their credit card bills, it is quite likely that they will not realize that they have a problem at all. It is this sneaky, almost unnoticeable quality about credit cards which makes them particularly precarious to their users.

Because while meeting minimum payments might be doable for a great many credit card debtors, very few could actually clear their credit cards if they really had to. And perhaps this is the easiest way to see if you have a credit card problem, quite simply, if you cannot clear your debt within a couple of months, then you have a credit card problem, and sadly thanks to the high interest rates, even the smallest debt will increase exponentially over time!

How modern society combined with the credit card industry repayment structure makes the prospect of gaining freedom from credit card debt an extremely difficult proposition!

Thanks to the many tie-ins between the finance industry and the retail industry, the temptation to sign up for finance deals, are everywhere. Just pick any mainstream store and you can either sign up for a store card or make a purchase on easy payment terms. Then of course there are home loans, home improvement loans, equity, lines of credit, personal loans and overdraft facilities.

Indeed even when you visit your local bank you will be assailed, by an assortment of advertisements, aimed at enticing you to sign up to some sort of loan or credit facility. And of course let's not forget our local supermarkets, which are also offering low interest offers on credit cards these days!

So wherever you go there is some finance offer being made available to you!

So What has this Easy Access to Finance got to do with Credit Cards?

Basically most credit card debtors do not use their credit cards in isolation. As a rule of thumb most credit card debtors either rack up credit card debt because of poor spending habits, whereby they do not stop to think about the debt, or because they are already having trouble paying back their other loans. For the majority of credit card debtors, their credit card debts really started to get out of control once their other loans began to get out of hand!

For example a credit card debtor may have say $5,000 on their credit cards due to various purchases over the period of a year or two. However they might owe tens of thousands on their other loans. After a while their repayments on their other loans start to get out of hand, then they find that even paying for groceries and gas becomes difficult. So what do you do if its ten days to payday and you have no cash on your person or in your current account? Well, you use your credit card of course!

However even a few months of using a credit card to pay for everyday expenses will turn that 5k credit card debt into a 10k debt, and just add some time and some interest to this and before you know it you are heading past the 15k mark!

So it must be remembered that credit card debts are not in isolation! If you are in credit card debt today, chances are that you are also under pressure from other debts as well. And this is where we see the relationship between credit card debt and societal pressure

Basically the society in which we live in is filled with temptations, temptation designed to get you and me and most people into a debt cycle. If things start to get really out of hand, it is the credit card(s) which usually come to the rescue. However, because of the low minimum monthly payments and double digit interest rates, the credit card debt will quickly get out of control!

Another factor which comes about as a result of our debt orientated society is that even if you manage to get out of debt, the temptation to return to a debt lifestyle is almost inexorable. If you have held credit card debt for some time now, more than likely you have undergone this regrettable experience of reducing your credit card debts, possibly even clearing them completely, only to find yourself falling right back into them all over again.

And this is the real tendency, not just of credit card debt, but of the entire societal structure which pushes us towards indebtedness. In particular credit cards represent a very tricky kind of debt, because they are really hard to clear, and out of all the debts which you are undergoing it is your credit cards which need to be tackled most aggressively!

So if you have a credit card debt problem, and perhaps have had a go at clearing this debt in the past only to find yourself right back at square one again, then it's not simply enough to just tighten your belt and reduce expenditure. Indeed it's not enough even to sign up with a debt relief company and seek credit card debt consolidation or settlement. Rather you have to get yourself off the credit card debt cycle!

How do You get Yourself Free of the Ensnaring Effects of Credit Card Debt?

To answer this question it is necessary to look back once again at the interrelationship between credit card debt and societal factors. Paradoxically, if you simply go with the flow in modern society, before you know where you are, you will find yourself knee deep in debt, of one kind or another! The only way then to avoid debt, whether it is credit card debt or any debt whatsoever, is to reprogram your life! It is necessary to delve deep into every recess of your lifestyle and begin to make some radical changes!

So what sort of changes am I suggesting?

Well, rather than fighting the endless temptation to get into debt, it is my suggestion to you to learn a few handy tactics which will help to make sure that you become debt free. Secondly I am further going to emphasize the need to replace your present financial value system, which is more than likely based upon reflex reaction, with a financial value system which will have you responding to your life rather than reacting to it. The model which I propose is called the five keys to debt freedom, and it consists of the following 5 strategies which will help you to redefine your financial existence:

The Five Keys to Debt Freedom

The First Key: A plan to stop accruing new debts on your credit cards, in order to put a stop to increasing indebtedness.

The Second Key: A plan to figure out just how much money is required to make ends meet, as well as following a program which teaches you how to live within a budget.

The Third Key: A plan to create a financial buffer zone so that you can protect yourself from most sudden financial setbacks, which would normally have thrown you back into credit card debt.

The Fourth Key: A plan to set up some new goals to strive for, and to start moving forward with your life, rather than focusing on endlessly putting out fires in your financial situation.

The Fifth Key: A plan to redirect the money which you have now saved yourself, from paying out on credit card debts, in order to build the lifestyle and long term security which you really want out of your life!

In a nutshell the emphasis with the 5 pillars is to begin by getting rid of your outstanding credit card debt, but more importantly it doesn't end there, rather it is equally important to redirect your financial expenditure towards wealth creation. Let's just think of it in terms of cycles of activity:

From Debt Cycle to Wealth Cycle

So far we have gone into considerable detail outlining the debt cycle which is so prevalent in society today and in particular the credit card debt cycle which is designed to keep you ensnared in a reactionary state of constant indebtedness. While it is very difficult to free yourself from the debt cycle, the biggest problem is not actually becoming free of debt but rather the biggest problem is in maintaining this debt Free State, simply because the temptation to become indebted is a constant in our modern lifestyle.

In particular most of us have terrible financial values!

How My Weak Financial Values have Cost
Both Myself and My Family a Great Deal!

I know in my case I was raised to be very conservative in how I spent money. "Neither a borrower nor a lender be!" my father used to always say to me, quoting Polonius from Shakespeare's play Hamlet. While in a way this was good advice, it didn't stop me from getting up to my eyeballs in debt!

How did this happen?

Well, my financial values where not very good. While I followed my father's advice and always tried to live within my means, the simple fact of the matter was that I had no idea about finances, about budgeting, about creating or following any kind of financial strategy. So while my intentions where always to live within my means, a period of time came whereby I suddenly had a lot of financial commitments.

I had a business which was struggling, and then at this time I got married, and for one reason or another my wife was not in a position to work, so I went from being a struggling bachelor to being a really struggling married man. We obviously had to live in a bigger apartment once we were married which cost more money and we had increased expenditure, yet my income was not going upwards to compensate. At this stage my financial problems began!

Roll on a year or so later and at this stage my wife was pregnant, and our finances where in a terrible state because by now my business was failing badly. We were taking huge financial hits each and every month, and when I mentioned our financial problems to our friends and relatives they just shook their shoulders as if to say "oh well"! I never felt so adrift in all my life!!!

So here is my case, of a man who always lived within his means and yet was in a struggling business and who had to take on aboard some new responsibilities which came with family life. I never lived recklessly, I never misspent my income, and yet here I was taking out new credit cards and using them to pay for my groceries!

At the worst point in this entire financial fiasco my credit cards repayments where in the order of $1,700 a month and my credit card debts peaked at $65,000!

I hadn't gone on any fancy vacations or dressed myself and my family in designer gear! Rather we lived very sensibly, by the code set down by my father and yet here we were with a huge debt problem!

Worse still whenever I read any articles on indebtedness or listened to any radio shows, or watched any TV shows which tackled the subject of indebtedness, the advice was always the same old crap about tightening your belt and living within your means! But what to do if for whatever reasons your income is impaired and your expenses are high? It's at this stage that I started to think seriously about my debt problems and debts in general, and how the usual generic advice really didn't cut the mustard anymore!

It also marked the beginning of a period of time when I and my two brothers, who were also struggling with their debt problems, began to have regular discussions about the subject of debt and what we were doing to clear our debts.

It is out of this troublesome period in my life that the concept of this book and the subsequent material represented in our website www.creditcarddetbsecrets.org began to formulate.

The reason why I am mentioning all of this is twofold, firstly to share with you my reality, that I too have been standing where you are standing now, that I too have had sleepless nights worrying about debts, and the feeling of utter frustration and helplessness, that no one understood my problem, that nobody either wanted to help, knew how to help or could help me!

Secondly, that the questions which arose in my mind at time do have an answer, and that rather than wasting years of effort, if you read on and apply the tactics outlined in this book, it is possible to literally save yourself years of hassle and tension!

If You are not in the Driving Seat,

Someone Else is Doing the Driving for You!

Throughout this book, there will be an emphasis on outlining the debt culture and debt cycle and how it tends to entrap all of us, also there will be a lot of technical detail, which is designed to help you to navigate your way around it.

While the detail may seem a little bit relentless, there is logic to it. Firstly, modern society is designed to ensnare the majority of individuals into a debt trap. This is exactly what happened to me and also to my brothers, maybe you have gotten into debt because of your recklessness, in which case you are in a better position than you realize, because all it takes for you is to stop being reckless.

However, the majority of individuals with credit card debts, and debts in general, end up in a state of indebtedness simply because they sleepwalked themselves into it. Modern society is designed to do just this to you, and it is necessary to become aware of it, in order to counter it. In simple terms, if you are not in the driving seat of your financial life, somebody else is and debt will be the outcome of this reality!

Secondly, because modern society is designed to ensnare the unwary it is necessary to take due precautions in order to clear off present debt and also to prevent a reoccurrence! This is exactly what happened to me and my family.

I sleepwalked into a debt trap, whereby in a confused state while undergoing a period of cash flow crises, I made ends meet with credit cards and the rest is history. The old World advice of tightening your belt and living sensibly worked just fine back in the 1970', the 1980' and even early 1990's. However you don't have to be a spendthrift to get into debt anymore! And belt tightening will not free you from this relentless debt!

Why it's not Enough Anymore

to Pay off Credit Card Debts

Even paying off all your credit card debts is not effective anymore, because no sooner have you one debt cleared than another enticement comes along and lo and behold you will find yourself back in debt all over again!

Basically it is essential to upgrade your financial value system, if you want to avoid stepping back into debt all over again! I can tell you in all fairness that getting free of debt is the least of your worries!

Most credit card debtors will either get free of their debts, or very nearly free of their debts, however, no sooner have they freed themselves then they will end up all getting back into debt once again. I have been there myself a few times, whereby I thought I had everything under control, only for the debt to set fire all over again, much like a bush fire catching fire just when it looked like it was going out!

So the only effective way to become debt free is not only to clear debt, but also to upgrade your financial value system!

So the reason for my indebtedness was because of my weak financial values. I am quoting my own story simply because weak financial values does not necessarily mean that you are spendthrift, rather it means that you do not know what you are doing, and that's the key!

You see for all my sensibility, I had landed myself in a business which was not very good and I had absolutely no leverage which could help to get me out of my difficulties. Getting married and suddenly having to look after my wife and then our son, would further complicate things because now I had even more outlay and my income was actually reducing at the same time, even though I was working 14 hour days, 7 days a week!

Where did I go wrong?

Well I should have picked a better business to begin with. But admittedly businesses can always go awry, however, I should have had some kind of financial reserve in place, whereby I had invested wisely when I did have some money.

Furthermore, once the business began to fall apart, which it did so over a period of years, I should have seen it coming, at that time I should have responded by looking into other ventures or even simply going back into a regular job. However, instead I moaned about it, but I never really did anything proactive, I simply reacted, and as we can see racking up huge credit card debts did not help one bit!

Importantly, I think I was expecting someone to help out, suggest something, do something, and yet no matter how much I complained about it, no one would do anything, foolishly I thought that my family and close friends would come to my assistance.

However, in reality we have to row our own boat when it comes to our finances. I was expecting too much from everyone else. They probably didn't take my moans and groans too seriously. However, eventually when everything completely melted down, and I had to leave my business, my family did come to my aid and help us out. But this only happened at time of complete financial failure! If I had responded rather than reacted, it never would have come to that in the first place!

So returning to the theme of weak financial values, the easiest way not only to escape the debt cycle, but also to stay free from it, is not to confront it but rather it is to replace one value system with another!

So if your financial values are weak (as in you don't know what you are doing) then society will do the thinking for you, and society at the moment is centered around debt, because the big players on the scene, the ones with all the marketing money are the finance companies and the very many retail companies, who are in cahoots with them!

I'm not knocking them, as everyone is entitled to earn an income, and they are not forcing you to become indebted, but the simply realty is that if you are not in the driving seat of your finances, then someone else is and they are looking for greater market share and greater market penetration. Just take a look at the graph below which outlines the profitability of the credit card industry:

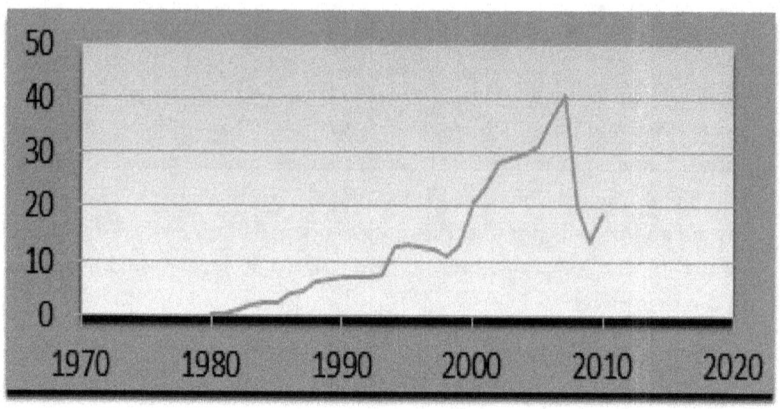

Chart 2 – Credit Card Industry Pre Tax Profits (1980 to 2007)

Yeah you haven't gone blind, its $41,000,000,000 (41 billion dollars) profit in 2007!

Ok the credit card industry has taken a hit since then, but it's a given that once the economy improves they will quickly regain at least a good chunk of that profitability!

So the easiest way to beat the system is to use the system to your advantage. This can be achieved by shifting from the debt cycle to the wealth cycle!

Let's put it this way, either way you spend money, however with the wealth cycle you spend money on medium to long-term investments which make you rich over time, and this is the key:

The Best Way to Stay Out of Debt is to Create Wealth!

If your bank account is full of money, it's kind of hard to be in debt now isn't it!

So the idea behind the 5 pillars is to lay down some structure, which you can follow, which will enable you not only to become free of debt, but also you will learn to reorient your finances so that you can start to accumulate wealth instead!

While the 5 pillars, when listed on paper may appear to be ridiculously simple, they are actually very powerful tools, and if you follow them, within a very quick period of time, you can turn your life around and move from the debt cycle into the wealth cycle instead.

Basically the society in which we live is ruled by all sorts of rules and regulations. The only difference between those who are in debt and those who are wealthy is how to leverage themselves within the financial system!

So, for example, the investor who has $5,000 invested in in a bond which returns 5% per year is obviously significantly better off than the debtor who is holding a debt of $5,000 on their credit cards at 15% interest per year. Both are in a spiral, both are deploying their money; just one is in a wealth cycle while the other is in a debt cycle!

Which Do You Want...
The Debt or Wealth Spiral?

Debt – Heading Towards $5,000 A Year In Debt Accumulation

Wealth – Heading Towards $5,000 A Year Savings & Investments & Debt Freedom

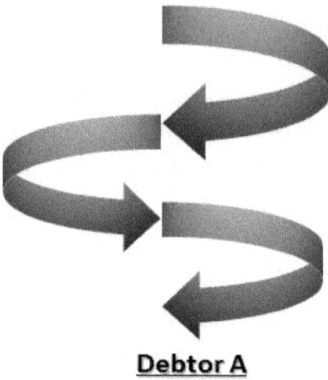

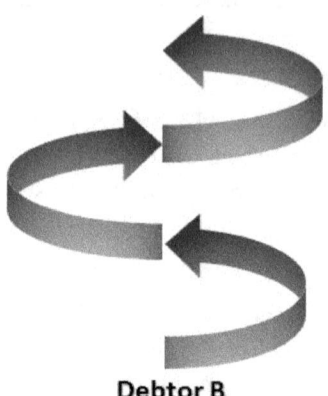

Debtor A

Debtor B

Debtor A and Investor B spends the same amount of money each year, and yet one is becoming wealthier year on year, while the other is becoming poorer. The same resources', yet simply by allocating them in a clever or stupid way produces either wealth or poverty over a period of time!

So needless to say we all want to be on the wealth cycle, so how do we go about it?

Let's begin with the first pillar to freedom from credit card debt!

Chapter Two – The First Key to Debt Freedom – Clear Your Debts

If you want to debt, you must stop accruing debt!

The first key to debt freedom is based on a very simple principal, whereby you get the debt reduction process under way simply, by making a determined effort not to accrue any new debt.

The reasoning behind this key is very simple, no matter what tactics you use in order to reduce credit card debt, the debt reduction cannot take place unless you put a stop to the debt creation cycle. The debt creation cycle follows simply and logically from the very structure of the debt system and in particular the credit card payment system, whereby the combination of low monthly payments and high interest rates, make it very difficult to pay off the debt principal, which in turn makes it difficult to reduce credit card debt.

While it is important to reduce all debts we shall focus in this chapter quite a bit on credit card debt as it is the most tenacious kind of debt.

Let's take a quick look at the rather enticing credit card repayment structure and how it is designed to entrap the unwary debtor:

- Low monthly minimum payments

- Double digit interest rates

- Minimum payment structure which is weighted towards paying of the interest rather than the debt principal

First off, low monthly minimum payments are designed to separate the credit card debtor from their hard earned cash! Basically the credit card industry average is to charge only 2% of this debt principal per month.

So if a credit card debtor has say $10,000 in outstanding debt, then their repayments will only be $200 per month. On one side it makes for easy payments per month, however, while the debtor is enjoying the benefits of only having to payback $200 per month on a $10,000 credit card debt, on the other side of the coin they are making absolutely no progress with clearing their debt principal!

This is where the other two factors come into play. First of all, double digit interest rates make sure that whatever amount remains on the credit card, quickly escalates. So in the example above the debtor with 10k in credit card debt may be getting away with a low monthly repayment but what's happening to their $9,800? Well it's escalating at double digit rates, which makes for a debt which isn't going anywhere!

Looking back at minimum payments, if a debtor with $10,000 in credit card debts and who has an average interest rate of 18% across their credit cards, if they only make minimum payments each month, it will take 7 years and 10 months years to clear their outstanding credit card debt, and that's only if they stop accruing new debts!

Think about it, how many people do you know who have $10,000 in credit card debt, and who are happy to make repayments of $200 a month for the next 7 years, without resorting to use their credit cards even once?

Not many, right!

This leads on to the final aspect of the credit card debt repayment structure, which is designed to keep the credit card debtor firmly with the debt cycle, and that's weighting the minimum payment towards paying back the interest rather than the debt principal.

While this is a common practice in most loans, it works fine in such things as a fixed period plan; however, it is really not good when applied to a loan which does not have a fixed term.

For example, if you take out a 20 year home loan, for the first 15 or 16 years, the greater part of your repayment will go towards servicing the interest on the loan rather than the loan itself.

Then the last few years are weighted towards making payments mainly towards paying back the debt principal. This is fine, because with a house you are either going to remain in the house, or you will sell it, either way it's ok. However, with credit card debt, the debt principal is changing all the time, so because of the dynamic nature of credit card debt, the repayment structure remains weighted towards paying back the interest rather than the debt principal.

Let's just take a look at the example of the credit card debtor, who has a debt balance of $10,000 on several credit cards, with an average interest rate of 15%. Initially, $150 is going to pay off the interest and only $50 is going to pay off the debt principal. However, by month 50, the payment order will have switched around to $150 being used to pay off the debt principal and $50 paying off the interest.

Now while that may work out ok with a fixed interest loan, with a credit card whereby the debtor adds new debts every month, the credit card will forever remain weighted towards servicing the interest on the loan rather than the loan principal. Just think about it this way, how many credit card users do you know who are willing to stop using the credit card for 7 or more years and simply making minimum payments on the loan as if it were a fixed rate loan?

Yep it never happens, credit card users, who are in the habit of only making minimum payments, keep on making regular purchases and simply hoping that the debt will go away.

Whereas, in reality as long as they keep on racking up debts on their credit cards, the minimum payment will never clear the debt. Rather, the credit card debtor is making sure that the credit card loan (for that's what a credit card is when it maintains a balance!) remains forever at the early stage of loan repayment, whereby the majority of the monthly payment simply goes to service the interest on the loan, rather than the loan principal!

If a credit card debtor pays back that $200 a month, they are only chipping away $50 per month for the debt principal!

Consequently, if a debtor adds $100 of new debt, even though they are paying back $200 a month, because only $50 goes towards clearing the debt, the debt principal actual increases month on month and the double digit interest rate make this figure increase exponentially over time.

This is why when we pay only minimum payments on our credit cards, the balance never reduces by a significant amount. You may well be thinking that you are doing well paying in 'x' amount of dollars per month, however, as long as you are making new purchases, no matter how small, you are effectively resetting the dial on your loan, so that the vast majority of your payment is merely paying off the interest on the debt!

I know it's a difficult concept to get your head around, but quite simply every time you add debt to your credit card, you are effectively resetting the debt payment, so that you end up forever paying back interest instead of clearing the debt principal!

It's a very shrewd repayment system, which has been devised by the credit card industry. A combination of high interest rates, low monthly minimum payments, and a minimum payment which is weighted towards paying back the interest rather than the debt principal, all add up to a debt which is never going to be reduced by minimum payments alone!

So, the first rule which we must remember, if we want to be free of credit card debt is that we must pay off more than the monthly minimum payments!

If you want to become free of credit card debt, the first rule is that you must pay back more than the minimum payments each and every month!

Hopefully, at this stage you are now convinced of the necessity of paying back more than the monthly minimum payments each and every month. Just remember, as long as you only pay back the minimum, the debt is not going anywhere, especially if you continue to make new purchases on your credit cards. And this is where pillar number one really comes into play.

Because the credit card repayment cycle, has been designed in just such a way that most, credit card debtors, simply make minimum payments and continue to make purchases on their credit cards. This is the sure fire way to create a credit card debt; and if you have debt on your credit card today, it is possibly a direct consequence off the sneaky nature of credit cards, whereby it's just so easy to make monthly minimum payments, and then to forget altogether about the debt principal.

Sadly, for a great many credit card debtors, it is only when they start having difficulty making those monthly repayments, that they investigate the debt principal.

A debtor might be having difficulty making a minimum payment of $1,000 a month, and then decide to look into it, only to find that they owe $50,000 in credit card debt, and let's face it, there are not very many people out there who could quickly clear a debt of this size, in a brief period of time!

More importantly, from the point of view of the credit card debtor who now wants to reduce their credit card debt, they have to stop accruing new credit card debt. Like we have seen earlier, just because a debtor makes a $200 minimum payment each month while only adding an extra $100 a month in transactions, do not think for one minute that their debt is reducing.

Rather, because of the weighting on the card, they are more than likely just paying back interest on the credit card. Furthermore, they are probably not actually either making headway on repaying their credit card debt, or they may even be increasing their credit card debt!

The important thing, to release, is that unless you can knock off a substantial amount of debt from your credit card debt each and every month, it will be impossible to clear your debt. By way of example, a debtor who spends $200 servicing a debt of $10,000 and who masses perhaps no new purchases each month, is still in danger of sliding backwards, because their debt is being cleared so slowly that even one or two new purchases per year, will knock the repayment plan out of kilter. And after a while, if a debtor see's no progress the tendency will be to slide back into old spending habits!

The Role of Inertia in Credit Card Debt

I am making a big point about this rather basic stuff, simply because while simple, it's just so incredibly important. The credit card industry has designed credit cards, in just such a way that, using them is far easier than taking cash out of your wallet or purse, and simply paying for things in cash!

The minimum monthly payment system, in particular, has been designed to keep you in a state of indebtedness because the credit card companies know only too well, that most of us are a little bit busy and a little bit lazy, so by default we end up in a state of debt!

Worse still, even when we want to clear our debts, it can be tempting to fall into the fallacy of believing, that if only we stop using out credit cards and keep on making minimum payments, that this will resolve our debts. Well, if that's your thinking, I am sorry to have to disabuse you, but at an average repayment timeframe of approximate 7 years (if you make minimum payments and don't make any new purchases on your credit cards), the chances of you slipping back into debt again are almost certain. I simply cannot state this in strong enough terms:

If you want to clear your credit card debt, you must stop accruing new debts, and the best way to do so, is to stop using your credit cards altogether!

This might sound harsh, but it's the simple truth!

As long as you are using your credit cards on a regular basis, no matter what efforts are being made to clear the debt, the debt will simply keep on coming back. Effectively, it's like having a hole in a bucket and wondering why the water keeps on disappearing!

So, even though you might be budgeting aggressively and even making concerted efforts to pay back more than the minimum payment, so long as you make purchases on your credit cards, the mixture of interest, and the weighting on the repayment system towards paying back the interest on the debt over and above paying back the outstanding debt principal, will all add up against your debt relief efforts!

Consequently, the only way to guarantee success is to, either stop using your credit cards altogether, or if you must, just retain one credit card and make a point of clearing the debt principal on it within the turnaround period.

The only sane way to use a credit card is to

clear the card completely within the turnaround period, which usually means clearing the

card each and every month!

Admittedly, it is difficult in this day and age to go without a credit card. However, by retaining just one credit card, it is easy to track it, and also by clearing whatever purchases you have made within the turnaround period, will mean that no new interest is being charged. This is the only sane way to use credit cards.

If you have to use a credit card, do make sure that you pay it back immediately, because once the debt balance stays on the credit card longer than a month, interest will start accruing, and so the debt cycle continues!

Also, it is very important to reduce credit cards down to one card. Most credit card debtors, slip into multiple credit card ownership, because it's a handy way of getting by, for a while! With most new credit cards, a period of low interest will apply, and for a great many credit card holders, who are having a difficult time making their monthly repayments, having a new credit card can help to relieve the burden for a while, that is until the special offer ends and the interest begins accruing all over again.

While there is certain logic involved in having so many credit cards, in the long term the idea of using special offers back fires, and in many cases it backfires badly, simply because so many credit cards, with special offers attached, actually have terrible payment terms applied once the special offer timeframe comes to an end. Of even greater importance, carrying multiple credit cards makes it very difficult to track your repayments. It makes it more difficult to see what your real debt balance is, and there is a tendency, to miss payments which comes with late fees and yes even more interest being charged!

So, do yourself a favour and just retain one credit card, and if you have to say make a purchase of $100 this month, then make a point of paying back this money this month!

What to do with the other cards?

Where possible, pay off the debt and return them; and if the debt is outstanding simply lock the credit cards away so that you don't see them and are not tempted by them!

The Role of Society and Personal Factors in the Accruement of New Credit Card Debt

Finally, if we want to stop accruing credit card debt, it is easy to simply blame the credit card companies; however, societal pressures also have a role to play as do our own personal inclination to spend money on our credit cards!

Societal pressure - Temptation to live like the Jones's:

We live in a society which tells us to spend, spend, and spend. It is difficult not to spend. And much expenditure, which used to be deemed as discretionary, is now seen as a necessity. For instance, the summer vacation and the Christmas festivities are bound to be expensive times for most folks. And, there is an inordinate amount of societal pressure to go out and spend some money. Whereas, our parents and our grandparents, would simply save until they could buy something, we have become brainwashed into buying today and then paying for it later on.

Now ,if you want to reduce credit card debt, and you find that your credit card debt balance is always static or only diminishing slowly, because of the debt repayment structure, as noted above, then it is always going to be difficult to reduce credit card debt. Because even when you make only small purchases on your credit cards, the debt principal begins to move upwards and not downwards, and because of this you are forced into spending most of your monthly payments, simply to service the interest on the outstanding debts

Personal Factor – Denial:

Denial is another factor which prevents credit card debt reduction from taking place. Because, as it is, there is a tendency for the credit card debts to remain practically the same, and of course they easily increase because of discretionary pressure.

However, on a personal level we are in denial of our credit card debt reality, and indeed we are in denial of perhaps all of our debts, such as overdrafts, auto loan, and home loan and so on, so it becomes an easier task to simple ignore the elephant in the room, rather than to do something about it.

You see the debtor who owes $5,000 and who wants to reduce credit card debt, knows that if their debts are increasing, even by a small amount, that they have a problem and must do something about it. And yet most credit card debtors, will wait until the problem gets out of hand, whereby they owe many thousands of dollars in credit card debt.

So, whatever your present level of debt is, at some stage earlier on it was a far smaller debt and would have been far easier to reduce credit card debt, if you had chosen to do that at an earlier time. The reason why you now have a big problem is because of denial. If you had not been in denial, you would have stopped accruing debt and achieved credit card debt reduction already!

So, in summary we can see that there is a litany of factors, both external, such as the credit debt payment structure and societal pressures, combined with the personal internal factor of denial, which have resulted in your present credit card debt problem.

I think it is fair to say that the majority, of credit card debtors, who have had a debt problem for a substantial period of time, have managed to reduce credit card debt, at some stage or another. However, the reason why the debt returns is, because the debtor merely deployed debt reduction tactics, without taking into account the debt creation cycle.

It does not matter whether, it is that they achieved a credit card debt reduction but still retained some balance on their cards and the balance began to accrue once more, or whether they achieved a zero balance, but then gave into societal pressure. Either way, as long as the debtor does not manage to break free, from this credit card debt creation cycle, then they have no long term possibility to achieve and remain in a state of credit card debt reduction!

The First Key to Debt Freedom Reduces Debt and Stops Accruing New Credit Card Debts & Loans

This is why the very first pillar of credit card debt freedom, is to stop accruing more debt on your credit cards. It is the first essential step, towards credit card debt reduction, and this makes it a very important step. It does not matter what tactics you use to reduce credit card debt, it will always end up coming back, unless you manage to escape from the credit card debt cycle!

The idea, behind the 5 pillars of credit card debt freedom, is that the root cause of your credit card debt problems is built upon ignorance of financial reality, combined with an addiction to the stress relieving aspects of spending money, and spending your way out of anxiety.

The 5 pillars will take you out of debt, and replace the vision of debt, with an aspiration to achieve a better life for yourself. In order to create a new abundant life, it is necessary, first of all to bring about a significant credit card debt reduction. And the firsts to step required to reduce credit card debt, is to free you from the credit card debt creation cycle.

While this may sound very difficult, all that you have to do at this stage is to either stop using your credit cards, or if you have to use them, make sure that you pay back into your account whatever amount you just spent. So, for example, if you buy your kids a pair of trainers for $100, then payback that amount before the credit card debt bill due! This way you will not accrue new debt, and you will make progress, however slow it may be in an effort to reduce credit card debt!

The simple act, of no longer accruing new debt on your credit cards, may not sound very exciting; however, it is the first vital step towards credit card debt reduction. The next stage or pillar will involve budgeting, whereby once you have stopped adding debt to your credit cards, you will then begin to learn how to free up some money, so that you can put some of that money back into the credit card reduction process, and quickly reduce credit card debt, once and for all.

Chapter Three - The Second Key to Debt Freedom - Budgeting & Debt Relief Programs

A plan to reduce debt by budgeting and to redirect this money into paying off credit card debt bills.

The second key, which leads you back towards credit card debt freedom, is budgeting. Now let's set the record straight, on budgeting, and its relevance to all strategies which are aimed at paying off credit card debt. Whether you conclude that your credit card debts are not too severe, and that you believe you can reduce debt on your own; or if you feel the need to join a debt relief program, such as a debt settlement or debt consolidation plan, regardless which option you decide to follow, budgeting has a role to play in paying off credit card debt.

The standard budgeting approach, which you will read about on the internet, involves following a series of strategies which reduce debt by spending less and saving more, and then diverting the money which has been saved into paying off credit card debt. While this is true, for debtors who are relying solely upon budgeting, it also has a role to play for any credit card debtors who are paying off credit card debt via a debt relief company.

For example, a debtor who is on a credit card debt settlement plan needs to come up with a one off settlement payment in order to clear their outstanding debts. So in this case, budgeting will help them to get this payment together more quickly than if they made no budgeting efforts at all.

Also, for a debtor who wants to consolidate their debts, with a debt management plan (DMP), they are amending their debt repayments by renegotiating the interest on their debts. Here too budgeting works to assist the process, because while reducing interest may save a few hundred dollars a month, another few hundred dollars can be saved via budgeting, and this money can be used to pay back the debts back more quickly.

Finally, even when you manage to clear your debts completely, budgeting still has a role to play simply because if you want to stay out of debt, then it is necessary to learn to live within your means, so as to prevent a relapse into debt!

Budgeting is not just a good idea; it's a vital strategy which will help you, not only in paying off credit card debt, but also in maintaining your newfound debt freedom!

Each pillar, in the pillars of credit card debt freedom, is vitally important if you want to reduce debt and remain debt free. In particular, budgeting as a way of paying off credit card debt is actually a very subtle technique. Because on the practical level budgeting will obviously help to reduce debt, because you free up some money and then you can roll over this money into debt repayment.

So, this is strikingly obvious, but what is less obvious is the role which budgeting plays in keeping this debt at bay. To gain a better understanding, of budgeting and its roll in paying of credit card debt and keeping it off, it is necessary to take a quick look at the causes of credit card debt.

While, some credit debtors end up in debt because of sudden unexpected expenditure, the majority of credit card debtors find themselves sinking slowly into debt over a period of time. As discussed in a previous pillar, the etiology of credit card debt is based upon four external forces and one internal force, which are:

- External causes of credit card debt:
- Low minimum payments
- Double digit interest rates
- Inverted interest to debt principal payment structure
- Societal pressure
- Internal cause of credit card debt:
- Denial

Now, by the time the credit card debtor attempts to reduce debt, they usually have two problems. Firstly, the enormous outstanding debt principal, and secondly the monthly minimum payments which end up getting out of hand. The debtor now has the problem, that they cannot clear the outstanding debt principal, nor can they meet the monthly minimum payments!

Of course, budgeting will help greatly, and for debtors who have serious debts which are way out of control, then they may also need to seek help in paying off credit card debt by engaging with a debt relief company.

But here is the thing; even if you reduce debt, even if you end up paying off credit card debt and are completely free of this debt, if you return to your old budgeting activity (or lack of it, we should say), then pretty soon you will end up in debt all over again!

The most important thing which I can tell you is not to fixate on the debt, but rather to fixate on changing beliefs and lifestyle habits, so that the debt will not return!

Believe me, if you are in debt today, you will manage to reduce debt and become free of it, it's just a matter of time and you will do it. But where nearly everyone gets stuck, is on the resumption of debt, because societal demands combined with our own denial mechanisms result in our re-accumulation of debt, often over and over again. Remember credit cards and indeed the personal finance industry is built upon the presumption that ordinary people cannot live without debt!

So, if you are interested in paying off credit card debt, but do not want to re-assume that debt at a later stage, then you are going to have to make significant lifestyle habit changes. And the single most important one is budgeting. Budgeting is not simply a case of living within your means, and saving some money, and using this money to reduce debt. While this is all true, from a bigger perspective, budgeting is about learning to change lifestyle and learning how to live within a certain frame work, regardless of societal pressure, financial mechanisms or inner compulsions!

The Nuts and Bolts of Budgeting and how it Fits in with the 5 Keys of Debt Freedom

To make the most out of budgeting, there are two aspects which have to be kept in mind. Firstly, on a practical level there are some useful budgeting tactics which you can use to reduce debt. However, on a second level, is the changing of beliefs and lifestyle habits, so that you reduce debt and stay out of debt forever.

Budgeting Tactics

Maintain a budgeting Diary:

This might sound like a difficult and boring task however, it is absolutely vital if you want to pay of credit card debt. Because, unless you know how much income you have and how much outgoings you have each month, it is simply not possible to make long term progress, in paying off credit card debt, especially if you want to stay debt free from now on.

While it may sound like a silly thing to maintain a budgeting diary, without it you will never know where your money is going!

Put it this way, on paper we may have enough money coming in each month in order to make ends meet, and yet each month we may well find ourselves going deeper and deeper into debt. This is a very common scenario for a great many people, and it is the atypical profile of many credit card debtors, who simply find their credit card debts are going upwards with each and every month!

It's not the monthly maintenance expenditure, which is plunging you and your family into debt, rather it is the one off expenditures which result in a spike in outgoings every month or two, which is resulting in the rapid accumulation of credit card debt!

If you maintain a budgeting diary, over the period of a few months, you will start noting down spikes in your expenditure, and with that you will start to understand where all your money is going! It is not the monthly maintenance expenses which plunge you into debt rather it is the one off expenditures, which come about every month or two which raise your out goings without it even being noticed.

For example, a credit card debtor may have an income of $2,500 per month, and on paper their outgoings, including credit card payments may, come to say $2,200 per month. So on paper they should have $300 left over, at the end of every month, and yet they may well find themselves not being able to make ends meet, and may even find at the end of the month, while they are awaiting their salary and that they have to use their credit card to buy simple things such groceries and gas.

So, instead of being up $300 per month, they find themselves going into debt by maybe $200 per month. This increase of debt becomes $2,400 over a year plus all the interest! So, obviously someone in this scenario is quite simply incapable of paying off credit card debt!

By maintaining a budgeting diary, this debtor would start seeing where their money is going, perhaps their auto insurance was up one month, and the next month they had to buy some presents for their kid's birthday! When you add up the outgoings over a few months, then you start to see where the money is going. So, in the above example the debtor may well find that they need $2700 per month to survive.

So our initial cash projections are always wrong, simply because we cannot take into account every sudden expense, which is going to crop up. However, by maintain a budgeting diary, over the course of a few months, the various substantial one off expenses will begin to be recorded, and a more accurate picture of financial expenditure will begin to emerge!

Now, you may be thinking, "well I don't need to keep a budgeting diary, I'll just check my bank account and see how much my monthly total expenditure is over a few months, and that way I will know how much I am spending on average." While this may sound logical, by checking your bank account every few months or so, you can gauge the total expenditure. However, you will not know where the money is going, which will make it very difficult to effectively reduce expenditure; and unless you reduce expenditure you will not be able to reduce debt!

Maintaining a budgeting diary is vital, so how long do you need to maintain the budgeting diary?

You do not need to maintain it forever, but you do need to maintain it during the debt reduction process. Indeed, even when you get clear off the debt, do maintain a watch on your finances, and run a check on it now and again, where you maintain a budgeting diary for a few months, once or twice a year.

I would advise this, even for the most affluent of people, even if you end up paying off credit card debt and are completely free with thousands of dollars in the bank, it is a good idea to check out your expenses now and again, and prune where necessary. Most people will allow their expenses to increase in a wasteful manner, unless they make a point of observing their outgoings. Consequently, even if you reduce debt and are financially comfortable, why waste money, when that money could be used for something more useful in your life!

Prune the excess expenditure:

Now here comes the moment of truth! Once you maintain the budgeting diary for a few months, you will come to realize two things. Firstly, you will have a reasonable idea as to how much money is required to make ends meet, each month. Secondly, you will begin to see wasteful expenditure. For example, maybe you eat lunch in a café every day, and it self-cost $5, so over 20 working days in a month, this adds up $100. So maybe if you made your own lunch and brought it to work you could feed yourself for $3 a day. So something this simple could save you $40 per month!

Multiply this, by several other minor modifications, and you may well find that you can easily save yourself $200 or $300 dollars a month, whereby this extra money can then be used to pay off credit card debt!

Also, this can be used to prevent a relapse into sudden reactionary credit card expenditure, because you have excess money in your current account, so that when sudden expenses come up, you do not have to reach for your credit card!

Are you a credit card debt gunslinger?!!! Do you reach for your credit card whenever something unexpected happens in your life?

Pruning is always an interesting exercise, because you have to make judgment calls, on where to reduce expenditure. Ok, maybe your rent is very high; possibly you could save a few hundred dollars a month, by moving to a cheaper location. Then again you have to balance this against other factors, for example maybe your kids school is very close to home, so it's a judgment call which has to be made. Unless you are living alone, the decisions which you make, in order to reduce debt, have to be signed off by all of the family members.

The important thing, to remember, is that if you have significant debt, then it will take time to pay off credit card debt. Even with the fast debt relief method, which is debt settlement, it will take a year or so, to reduce debt. With other methodologies, such as credit card debt consolidation and budgeting, it will usually take several years.

So, while it is a great thing to get stuck into the debt reduction process, you have to be able to sustain it otherwise it will get derailed. Because if you take draconian measures, to save money, maybe you might drive your family crazy! So remember, slow but sure, steady realignment of your debts is the way to go!

Reduce Debt with Budgeting or

Join a Debt Relief Program?

As noted earlier, regardless which debt relief strategy you end up pursuing, budgeting has to be a part of it. However, you do need to make up your mind as to which way to go. At this stage, after weighting up your outgoings, making some effort to prune unnecessary expense and then comparing this against your income, you should be able to gain some clarity regarding your debts.

So, if you want to reduce debt simply by following a budgeting plan, then it is necessary for you to be able to settle up your all your debts within a few years, otherwise you are wasting your time. For example, if you owe $25,000 and your monthly payments are $500, and after pruning your debts, you see that you can make this $500 payment plus you can plough an additional $500 per month into paying of credit card debt, and then get going with debt reduction by budgeting.

However, if say you prune your debts and are still not making enough even to make the minimum payments, then it is a ridiculous idea to even attempt to reduce debt via budgeting!

In this case you have to consider either credit card debt settlement or credit card debt consolidation. Of course, you can assist these debt relief strategies via budgeting, but budgeting will only act as a form of assistance with these methodologies.

Finally, regarding which debt relief methodology you take up, the best way to select either debt settlement or debt consolidation, is to think in terms of repayments.

If your interest rates were reduced slightly, would you be able to make the payments?

If so, go for credit card debt consolidation, as a way of paying off credit card debt. However, if even with reduced interest rates, you cannot make the payments, then you should consider credit card debt settlement instead!

Get rid of your credit cards: As noted, in the first pillar of credit card debt freedom, it is vitally important that you refrain from accruing new debts, on your credit cards, whilst you are undergoing the debt reduction process. This is terribly important, because the debt repayment structure is designed in such a way that if you keep on making purchases on your credit cards, and only making minimum payments, that it becomes impossible to reduce the outstanding debt principal.

So, with that in mind, the easiest way to resist temptation is to get rid of your credit cards, or at least most of them. I know that in this day and age it is almost a necessity to have at least one credit card, so if you feel the need to hold onto one credit card then keep one card, but payback any expenditure almost immediately. So if you make a purchase today, make a point of paying off credit card debt within the 50 to 60 day interest free period, and do make a point of only using your credit card when absolutely necessary!

Snowballing:

If you sign up, to a debt relief program, then snowballing will not be necessary, since you can reduce debt simply by following either the debt settlement or debt consolidation plan. However, if you are interested in paying off credit card debt by budgeting alone, then snowballing is a necessary tactic, which will help to reduce credit card debt in a faster turnaround time.

Basically, with snowballing you pick out the credit card, either with the lowest balance or with the highest interest rate, and make a point of paying it off first while only paying off minimum payments on the other credit cards. Once you have paid off this credit card, you simply roll over this money to the next credit card and so on.

By snowballing, you will knock off a few months from the debt reduction timeframe. There is no additional expense, rather you simply take a tactical approach to paying credit card debt. So since it will cost you no money to do this, it is a must for you to deploy snowballing in order to reduce credit card debt.

Learn to say no:

So far, we have looked at practical budgeting debt relief pointers, but do not forget the big picture, whereby you have to alter beliefs as well as habits.

Practical suggestions, such as maintaining a debt diary and snowballing, make sense even if you have to think about them and how you are going to integrate them into your debt reduction program. However, it is the bigger picture, that subtle scenario of our financial beliefs and habits which are of even more fundamental importance, if you want to end up paying off credit card debt quickly.

One vital strategy to help you, to reduce credit card debt, is simply to learn how to say no!

What does this mean? Well if you have done your homework and you now know how much income you have, how much monthly expenditure you have, and what strategy you are following in an effort to reduce debt, and then you have to keep to it!

In our present society, we are surrounded by constant temptations to go out and spend, spend, spend! Simply put, if you really want to reduce debt and finish with paying off credit card debt, and you want to be free of debt forever, then you have to select to live a debt free life, which means saying no sometimes.

Sometimes, you might have to say no to the guy in the shopping mall selling you something. Sometimes, you will have to say no to a family member who wants to carry out some unnecessary discretionary expenditure; and sometime you will have to say no to your own comfort spending. Whatever it is, you simply have to stick with the plan, if you want to reduce debt, and learning to say no is a core element to the budgeting success plan!

Integrating Budgeting into a Debt Reduction Plan

If you are interested in paying off credit card debt, and once clear of this debt you want to stay free of it, then budgeting has a role to play. In the points raised above we have outlined the nuts and bolts of budgeting, of how it can help you to reduce debt regardless of which debt relief method you decide to take up. So far we have outlined some useful strategies to help reduce debt, with budgeting, such as maintaining a diary, getting rid of credit cards, and learning to say no.

While these are all valid tactics, the reason why budgeting is the second pillar behind credit card debt freedom, is because of the macroscopic factors, which arise with budgeting. If budgeting was simply a series of tactics, it would not have a really big role in the debt reduction process. However, it is because budgeting effects every aspect of our lives, that it is so important.

You see even if you are in debt today, you will eventually end up paying off credit card debt, but for how long?

Finding your Financial compass!

Unless you change some financial beliefs and lifestyle habits, the debt will surely come back all over again. Where budgeting can help you to reduce debt and stay free from it forever, is in the perspective which it gives you, so that you know how much income you have and you know how much expenses you have. It's like having a financial compass in your hands, while with a physical compass true north always points upwards, by the same token with the financial compass of budgeting, you know that the way to reduce debt, and to stay free of it, requires that you follow the true north of a balanced financial statement.

Which means, that you know how much, you can spend per month and you stick to that, regardless what everyone is suggesting you spend your money on, regardless of your own inner temptation, you simply stick to your monthly budget!

This is the greatest reward which comes about as a result of conscientious budgeting, that you discover your financial true north! It becomes a case of no longer having to guess your way through the morass of financial decision making! Rather, once you come to terms with the accurate realities of your finances, you will be able to make objective financial decisions. Furthermore, this isn't simply a one trick pony; rather it can be adapted as you journey throughout your life. The numbers may change, but the financial principles will remain the same!

When you get into budgeting, and making it an aspect of your belief systems and lifestyle habits, you simply get into the habit of makings sensible financial decisions, and this is why budgeting is the second pillar to credit art debt freedom!

It's very easy to read about budgeting, and to think about having a go at it, however, unless you have a workable template which you can follow, it is difficult to pull it off. So let's take a look at budgeting in action via some helpful budgeting templates which will help you make progress with the budgeting process.

Budgeting Templates

Just take a look at the sample budgeting template below. In this sample template we are looking at the budgeting efforts of our mythical couple John and Verona Ricardo. The Ricardo's are not real people; rather they have been created, as a means of illustrating the vagaries of financial planning. Whereas, simply throwing statistics and principals at you it would become confusing, instead by creating an imaginary family, it will be easier to follow the principals which are to follow.

For the sake of convenience, the Ricardo's are a reasonably well-heeled middle class family, of husband and wife team, John and Verona, and their two kids. Their income and debts are middling, however don't get hung up on the details.

From my experience the Ricardo's could just as easily have been very poor or very wealthy. Because debt knows no stranger! It is possible for anyone to fall into debt. Certainly it is easier to fall into debt if you are poor, because of a lack of expendable income, but then again the wealthy can accumulate far greater debts in a far faster turnaround period, so take your pick, debt is awful whichever way you look at it!

So instead of getting hung up by the sample figures, just adjust accordingly, and imagine that I am talking about you, your family and your personal financial conditions, that way you will get on just fine!

The first part of the template lists the Ricardo's various credit card debts, followed by their income, after taxes. When listing income, it is vital to list take home income, because you can only spend that which you receive in your hand. Also with this template, the debts go right to the top of the page, that way they are forefront in our mind.

The next few sections list the various deductions, such as minimum payments, money set aside to pay off debts, money set aside as a financial buffer and fixed outgoings. So what do all of these sections entail?

Minimum payments:

Unless you have set your mind on taking up with credit card debt settlement, in which case you will be withholding payment to creditors, you will have to make your monthly minimum payments. Even if you decide to take up with debt consolidation, minimum payments will still have to be made, the only difference being that with consolidation you make the payment to the debt relief company.

So if there is one thing which we have emphasized, so far, is the necessity of paying back more than minimum payments, if you want to clear your debts. So the first part of paying back more than minimum payments, is to make a determined point of paying back the minimum payments regardless of what is happening. On a month by month basis, the average credit card delinquency rate fluctuates between 2.5% to 3.5% of credit card holders, so even on a good month around 4 million Americans (3), do not manage to make their minimum payments!

Now, if you are serious about clearing your credit card debt, then it is absolutely vital that you make those minimum payments each and every month. Because apart from the tendency to backslide into debt, the other reality is that a late payment comes with a penalty against you, so now you have the debt, the interest and the late penalty to deal with!

Controlling credit card debt is difficult at the best of times, so do yourself a favor and make a point for putting money aside at the start of the month so as to pay off your minimum payments prior to all other household bills!

Money set aside for paying off debts:

Is quite straightforward, it simply represents the amount of money which you want to use each month to set aside and clear the debts. So if you are budgeting, then it's a matter of setting aside a set amount each month over and above the minimum payments in order to clear your debts. And this remains the case whether you are budgeting, or are on a debt settlement or debt consolidation program. Whatever way you look at it, you need to get some money together!

For example, if you are budgeting, then you need to pay over and above the minimum payments, in order to clear the debts. If you are on a debt settlement program, you need to amass enough money so as to make a one off debt settlement, so once again some money needs to be set aside. Finally, if you want to take up with a debt consolidation program, unless you want to remain on the program for several years, it is necessary to amass some money and make an effort to clear the debts more quickly!

By making a point of setting aside this money, there is absolutely no temptation to spend the money on other things!

Financial buffer:

This will be outlined in greater detail in pillar number 3, for now it's enough to know that you need to set some money aside to create a financial buffer. The theory behind this buffer is simple; basically many debtors get thrown of course when a sudden expense comes along, resulting in months of good work going to waste, because they have to put these one off expenditures onto their credit cards, in an effort to clear any extraordinary expenses.

We see an example of this in the sample budgeting template here below. Here we see a car repair, which costs the Ricardo's $435. As it happens they are able to cover the expense via their income, however, if they did not have this $435 in their bank account, then what would they do?

Most credit card debtors, would simply reach for their credit card and end up sliding backwards with their debts, however, with the financial buffet account, sudden unexpected expenses are taken care of. For more detail on this just take a look at pillar number 3.

Fixed Outgoings:

Fixed outgoings are there simply for your convenience. Basically we all have a certain set of expenditures which do not vary from one month to another. Things like rent or mortgage repayments, prepaid phone and TV plans and the like are included here. The advantage of listing these items at the start of the month is that it helps to establish just how much money is available for spending through the month.

Maximum allowable expenditure this month:

This is a simple limit based upon adding up all the household income and then deducting the minimum payments, money set aside to pay off the debts, the financial buffer fund and the fixed outgoings. What is left at this stage is the discretionary spending balance, which you can use through the month.

So in the sample example of the Ricardo's, after all deductions they are left with $3773 to do with as they will. So these include everyday expenses like groceries bills, petrol for the car and all other expenses such as entertainment etc.

On the face of it, the maximum allowable expenditure per month, sounds like a lot of money, but the idea behind it is that by taking out all necessary expenditures and one off expenditures that you are left with good ideas as to what you can spend on a particular month, without having to worry about going into debt.

In the Ricardo's case the figure is $3773, which sounds like a huge amount, but do remember that this is the sum of all their discretionary expenditure; it has to cover all general outgoings for the month. The important thing is that they only have to fixate on this figure, because they have already set aside money for their debts, rent and other expenses at the very beginning of the month. So it's like counting calories, however with the budgeting template you simply deduct the outright expenses and what you are left with is your discretionary expenditure, which you can enjoy throughout the month!

The basic idea behind this first page of the budgeting template, is not to provide some amazing debt relief solution, rather it's a simple way of helping you to see the wood for the trees. The example given is purposefully directed at a fairly affluent couple with a combined after tax income of $8,200.

The reason for this is twofold; first of all, even fairly affluent people have debt problems. While this couple has an 8k a month income, they have an outlay of $1177 a month just to make the minimum payments, so that's before they pay their rent or put food on the table!

Secondly, in the example which is given we can see how a family, with high overheads and considerable debts, can still manage to have a nice lifestyle while clearing their debts!

If you look further down the budgeting template sample, the second section is a table which the debtor can fill in as they work their way through the month (an empty template is included in the resources section). As we can see in this sample, the Ricardo's are living well. They attend ballgames, parties and the cinema on a regular basis.

Ok, in this example they have a good income too, but the point to take on board here is not the level of income, rather they know at the beginning of the month that they have a maximum discretionary expenditure of $3773, so as long as they keep their expenditure within this limit everything is fine.

Wouldn't you like to know at the beginning of the month, just how much you can spend and enjoy spending on discretionary items, without having to worry about going into debt; and feeling satisfied that even though you and your family are enjoying yourselves that your debts are reducing with the passing of each and every month! Remember, it's not about the money, if say your discretionary income is only $800 a month, and then work with that!

Rather it's about finding out just how much money you have to live on every month and sticking with it. Whether your income is large or small, there are pros and cons. If your income is low it will be difficult even making ends meet at all. If for example you fill in the budgeting template and find out that it is not possible to make ends meet, while putting money aside so as to pay of your debts, or maybe it's not possible even to make ends meet at all, then in this case you will have to consider taking up it some kind of debt relief option.

Do You Know Where Your Leaks Are?

On the other side of the coin, if your income is fairly good or even large, it can actually be really easy to spend vast amounts of money and yet be surprised to see your debts increasing each and every month. For people in this situation the budgeting template works well because it helps to isolate expenditure! Either way once you know where your financial leaks are you can do something to plug the leak!

For example in this sample, the Ricardo's make ends meet even while paying back minimum payments, putting money aside money to pay off debts and living a fairly nice lifestyle. At the end of their month, they are still within $37 of their discretionary expenditure limit, and strictly speaking their car expense could be covered by their financial buffer fund if they had to do so. But what if their expenditure was say a $1,000 over their discretionary expenditure limit? Well in that case, all they have to do is to take a look down the list of expenditures and see where it's all going wrong.

By filling in the budgeting template every month, it is easy for them to track their fixed expenditures, their debt expenditure and their discretionary expenditure. So they can easily see where their financial leaks are. So maybe if they were spending $ 300 a week on socializing, at least they can see it for what it is, and reduce it as necessary!

Where most debtors go wrong, is not in their lacking an income, but rather in their inability to manage their expenditure. At the risk of repeating myself, all I can say is that unless you have significant funds in the bank, each and every month and your long term assets are steadily increasing, then it is necessary to maintain a budgeting diary.

It really doesn't matter if you earn 10k a year, 30k a year or 300k a year. All that matters is your ability to make ends meet. And don't think that, just because you got a fat pay rise recently that, this entitles you to spend like a crazy man or woman. In reality regardless of income, most people simply live up their income. People, who earn 300k a year for example usually, live in neighbourhoods populated by other wealthy people and they spend accordingly!

So don't forget budgeting, if you know what's good for you!

Finally, as we can see by looking at the budgeting template, a budgeting diary is not a little black book with a few scribbles in it; rather it's a technical tool and should be treated as such. As we can see, in the sample, the Ricardo's list downs all their expenses, regardless how big or small. This is the real key to success, because, as noted earlier the main challenge with trying to live within ones means lies in the unpredictability of our outgoings.

So on paper they could easily live on their 8k a month after tax income, subtract their fixed assets and their minimum payments and they would still have nearly 5k left over. So it would be all too easy for them to conclude that their living expenses must be well within 5k, so why not spend as they feel fit and simply pay off a $1,000 a month, from their outstanding debts at the end of the month?

However, without keeping a budgeting diary, it becomes all too easy to simply spend, spend, spend, and before they know where they are, the Ricardo's, in this example and you in reality, could easily find themselves having spent the 5k and having added some more debt to their credit cards, and being completely unable to pay even their minimum payments by month end!

So no $1,000 cleared from their debts, rather more debt than ever, so what has gone wrong?

Without a budgeting diary, it's simply too easy to spend!

Just look at the Ricardo's budgeting dairy and we can see that while they are living a comfortable lifestyle, they are not living a flash lifestyle. This is a good example of a middle income household with a nice lifestyle but not a flamboyant lifestyle!

Date	Expenditure Type	$	DATE	Expenditure Type	$
11/01/2012	groceries	75		Ball game	60
11/02/2012	movies	50		snacks	40
11/03/2013	Lunch out	25		Dinner out	70
	groceries	125		Birthday present	27
	sundries	27		Charity donation	50
11/05/2012	School uniform	50		Cinema tickets	45
	shopping	200	11/24/2012	Lunch out	35
11/05/2012	pizza	15		DIY items	135
	Golf outing	115		groceries	12.5
	pizza	45		Train tickets	44
	drinks	75		Lunch out	35
11/15/2012	groceries	100		snacks	25
	petrol	200		sundries	50
	Car repair	435		groceries	110
11/16/2012	lunch	5		petrol	40
	sundries	17.5		Bicycle tires	20
11/17/2012	haircut	15		lunch	15
	Clothes shopping	56	11/25/2012	lunch	20
11/20/2012	socializing	80		Dry cleaning	40
	TV repair	50		Bin charge	30
	petrol	70		Renewed TV subs	110
	sundries	38	11/26/2012	swimming	20
11/21/2012	snacks	30		snacks	30
	Vet fees	75	11/27/2012	petrol	40
	Hair salon	120		grocery	9
	sundries	42	11/29/2012	Lunch out	25
11/23/2012	plumber	172		sundries	40
	petrol	140		New carpet	120
	Expense Totals	$2,447.5		Expense Totals	$1,297.5
				Whole Month expenses	$3,745

So without going crazy, they are spending their way through nearly $4,000 a month in discretionary expenditure. How difficult do you think would it be for them to spend $5000 instead of $4,000?

Probably pretty easily, at today's prices it's really easy to spend money!

Think of it this way, in the example of the Ricardo's, on $8,000 a month they are living well and paying $1,000 a month towards debt clearance. However, $1,000 more expenditure and they break even and $2,000 more expenditure and they go into another $1,000 of debt. To spend $1,000 in a 28day month only requires an expenditure of $35 a day, yeah that's amazing isn't it, just think about it $35 a day between debt and living nicely! And to spend $2,000 it only requires an expenditure of $70 a day!

For most individuals, they could easily spend this sum of money on social occasion or possibly eating lunch out a few times a week!

The point is that the difference between accumulating debt and clearing debt is far closer than you may realize. So by maintaining, a budgeting dairy, it will help you see the wood for the trees. In particular, while our average monthly expenditure may be approximately the same from one month to the next, one thing which maintaining a budgeting diary does is it reveals to us the expenditure which is not obvious, like the car repair for example.

And remember if it wasn't the car it would be something else, such as the school fees, a family reunion perhaps or a new suit for work. One way, or another, something out of the blue comes up nearly every month, so by maintaining a budgeting diary, it allows you firstly to start accounting for these one offs, so maybe you have school or college fees every 3 months, and have never thought about it before. So by becoming aware of it, at least you can start to get some idea, as to your average monthly expenditure.

Secondly, if a sudden expenditure comes up you can also deal with it. In the Ricardo's case, they had a car repair which cost them $435. Now, as it happens, this could be paid for out of their financial buffer fund. However, while the buffer fund will help, ultimately the buffer fund has to be topped up again, so ideally you don't want to dip into the buffer fund in the first place. So, in this example, maybe the Ricardo's would have had a few more families days out, maybe they have held themselves back a little in order to keep within their discretionary expenditure figures.

And this is the final thing to take from the budgeting diary concept. It takes a little bit of discipline and self-restraint. It takes self-discipline to maintain the diary, in the first place, and it also requires some self-restraint to live within the financial limits, which are revealed by the diary making. In the sample below, the Ricardo's live fairly well, but they do live within their discretionary expenditure limit, and that's the vital thing!

Subsequently, if you want to progress with budgeting (that means me, you and everybody, save for a few very wealthy types), you should maintain a budgeting diary. It means that you will have to show some self-discipline, and even a little restraint. However, as the example shows it does not mean that you have to live like a miser!

Let's say, for example you have a family reunion coming up in a months' time, and between traveling expenses, hotel fees and several social events it looks like it will cost a couple of thousand dollars. Then rather than blowing all the money on your credit cards, instead you can plan for it ahead of time!

Another famous example is Christmas; most families spend a fortune in Christmas and gather some debts along the way, well, be ahead of the posy, and plan for it ahead of time!

Budgeting does not have to be painful; it simply has to be rigorous in order for it to work for you!

And do remember that the difference between, accumulating debt and clearing it, is simply the difference between a few minor financial transactions per month. If you are having difficulty making ends meet, at the minute, just follow the steps set down, in this pillar, and start to apply them in your life and you will be surprised by the amazing turn around in your finances within a couple of months!

Finally, while budgeting is a great way to reduce debt, it is only one aspect of the 5 keys. Budgeting creates a space, a space which will help in paying off credit card debt, but there are other temptations, such as the temptation to walk back into debt simply because you are unprepared for sudden financial setbacks!

In the, next key to debt freedom, we shall look at a strategy to help you to plan ahead, so that no matter what is happening you will still be able to reduce credit card debt!

Chapter Four - The Third Key to Debt Freedom - Create a Financial Buffer Zone

A plan to create a financial buffer zone, so that you can protect yourself against sudden financial setbacks, and so keep the debt reduction process moving forward, so that it becomes a given that you will become debt free!

So far in pillars one and two, we have been speaking about the importance of keeping yourself on track, with the debt reduction process, by making sure that you do not accrue new credit card debt. We have also mentioned the necessity of maintaining a budgeting diary and making sure that you do stick to your budget. These two factors are really important, if you want to get debt free. So regardless of which debt reduction strategy, that you take up so that you can become debt free, whether it be budgeting alone or debt settlement or debt reduction, it is equally vital to keep away from new debts and to follow a strict budgeting program, in order to achieve the debt reduction results which you require.

However, while the first two pillars initiate the debt reduction process, it is really important to continue on with the other pillars so that you not only manage to become debt free, but also that you manage to stay free of debt forever. In particular, the third pillar is really important in the sense that it protects you against sudden setbacks. The third pillar simply consists of creating a financial buffer zone, whereby you apply the previous tactics mentioned in pillar one and two, both to reduce expenditure and also to create a financial buffer too, which will make sure that your debt reduction process is moving forward according to schedule.

The Importance of a Financial Buffer Zone

in the Debt Reduction Process

Most credit card debtors manage to make some inroads into their debts, from time to time. Also if they apply the strategies mentioned in the first two pillars, they will be well on the way to becoming debt free, because these strategies help the debtor to keep moving forward. By not accruing new debts, they are creating a financial surplus via their budgeting efforts.

However, it is equally important to create a financial buffer zone, because a great many debtors fall off the debt reduction wagon, simply because a sudden financial setback comes their way. Consequently, they end up reaching for their credit card or asking the bank for an extension on their overdraft facility, in an effort to deal with the financial blow which they have suddenly received.

If this has happened to you, then you know what I am talking about. Everything is moving forward, it looks like soon you will become debt free, and then suddenly without warning a crisis develops and you end up losing all the ground that you have made, and so you end up back where you started all over again!

However, while there is no way to insulate yourself from every potential setback, at least by applying little bit of prudence to the situation, it is possible to have a financial buffer zone in place which will insulate your debt reduction process from most sudden nasty surprises.

How much money should I put into my financial buffer?

This is a really good question, because the whole idea of a financial buffer is to have enough money set aside in order to protect the debt reduction process. However if you have too much money set aside, the debt reduction process will end up suffering, because that money could have been better spent towards clearing those outstanding debts.

There is no generic answer, which I can give you, because everybody has different circumstances to deal with.

For example, a bachelor living at home with his parents, and who has no dependents, will be able to get away with a far smaller buffer zone than a lone parent with one income, who is in a house or apartment with high rent or a high mortgage, and who has several dependents to look after.

Needless to say, a credit card debtor who has a mortgage and several kids at school and college may easily have a monthly expense figure, which heads into the thousands of dollars per month range; whereas the bachelor who lives at home may be able to get by on less than one thousand dollars per month.

So if we think in terms of having enough money set aside to last a couple of months without need for any income at all, for the bachelor the figure is quite doable, whereas with the example of the lone parent, it may be a quite colossal figure, which would be a waste of money which would be better served in paying off some outstanding credit card debts.

So, while it is ideal to set aside enough money to cover all of your outgoings for a month or two, in order to protect the debt reduction process, in reality even if you just have enough to cover a couple of months repayments, this will be enough to at least stop you having to reach for your credit card during most emergencies!

Let's put it this way, if you have enrolled in some form of debt reduction scheme and you need to set aside say $1,000 a month, so as to make the payments on the debt reduction process. Then if you can simply have an equivalent amount of money in an account, which has being specially set up for the purposes of being a financial buffer zone, then this will be enough to insulate the debt reduction process from most external factors.

While even having enough money set aside, to cover a couple of month's repayments on your loans, may sound like a lot of money, in actuality it is worth the effort. Put it this way, you want to become debt free, and you are making progress on your debts, then all of a sudden something pops up; maybe one of your kids has to get a new outfit for their sports activity and it ends up costing a couple of hundred dollars, or perhaps you spring a leak in your roof and it cost a thousand dollars to fix. It really doesn't matter what the sudden emergency is, rather what counts is that if you only have just enough money to cover your debt reduction program, and then a crisis breaks out, what are you going to do about it?

If you are totally unprepared, chances are that you will simply slip back into old habits and slap the expense onto a credit card, which solves the initial problem, but ends up putting you back into the debt roller coaster ride all over again!

Whereas a debtor, with enough money to make two months of repayments, can have a sudden financial setback and simply dip into this financial buffer fund, and they are still on course with their debt reduction process!

The Financial Buffer Zone Strategy in Practice

So what's the best way to create and operate a financial buffer zone in such a way that it protects the debt reduction process?

Decide on the amount of money which you need to keep aside.

First off, decide on the amount of money which you need, in order to protect approximately two months' worth of debt reduction repayments. While, this will not protect the debt reduction process, from all possible financial setbacks, at least it will provide a reasonable level of cover.

Set up a bank account which is dedicated as a financial buffer

There is absolutely no point in setting money aside, in an effort to protect the debt reduction process, and then simply keep the money in your regular bank account for this purpose, whereby there will be a constant temptation to dip into this reserve. In this situation, the old adage applies "out of sight, out of mind"!

Think about it this way, if you cannot see it, then you cannot spend It.! So, open up an account which is assigned especially for this purpose. Also, ideally set up an account which provides some interest, but which is flexible enough that you can make withdrawals from time to time. This way you can provide the level of support which you require, while getting some return on the money.

If you make a withdrawal, make a point of refuelling the account as soon as possible.

If you want to get debt free, then it's really necessary to refuel this account, as soon as possible, once you find yourself dipping into it.

So, for example, say you spent $1,000 on fixing your roof, and then make a plan to refuel the account over a reasonable period of time, such as 5 months at $200 per month. If that's a bit of a financial stretch, then just make it $100 per month. The point isn't to kill yourself, as you try to refuel the account, but rather that you make sure that if another nasty surprise comes along that you have a reasonable chance of avoiding a relapse into accruing credit card debt.

If we look back at the sample budgeting template in Pillar number three, the Ricardo's had a sudden one off expense of $435, which they had to make on a car repair. Now in the example cited, they did not have to dip into the Financial buffer Fund, but if they had to then in what way would it have panned out?

Basically by following, the suggested formula, of maintaining enough money so as to ensure two months minimum payments, the Ricardo's would have to have $2354 in the account, that's two months minimum payments! So in reality they would probably round it up to $2,500, maybe a little bit more, if they found this to be comfortable.

If they had to spend around $500 on a car repair, then it would be topped up in 5 months, at their present rate of $100 per month, which they have set aside for this financial buffer account. So, basically they don't have to do anything; rather they simply have to keep on maintaining their deposits in this account.

Let's put it this way, if they retain a balance of $2,500 and on a given month they spend $500, they will still have $2,000 in the financial buffer account, so that should cover most eventualities.

In reality every month or two, something will come up, and that's why we are suggesting that you make a deposit every month, unless the balance goes over the balance which you want to retain. Just take a look at the sample financial buffer account below, it will provide an idea as to how a financial buffer account will work in day to day life!

Ricardo Family Sample Buffer Account

January to December 2013

Month	Comment	Credit	Debit	Balance
January	No payment made because the account is in a positive balance of more than $2,500, or 2 months minimum payments!			$2,500
February	Withdrew $350 to cover sister's wedding		$350	$2,150
March		$100		$2,250
April		$100		$2,350
May		$100		$2,450
June		$100		$2,550
July	No payment made because the account is in a positive balance of more than $2,500, or 2 months minimum payments!			$2,550
August	No payment made because the account is in a positive balance of more than $2,500, or 2 months minimum payments!			$2,550
September	No payment made because the account is in a positive balance of more than $2,500, or 2 months minimum payments!			$2,550
October	Withdrew $2200 to cover medical bill. The bill was $2,700 in total!!!		$2200	$350
November		$100		$450
December		$100		$550

So we can see, in the example of the Ricardo's, that they only made ten deposits over the course of the entire year, because once the balance, of two months minimum payments ($2,500) had been reached, there was no need to go any higher than this.

Also we can note that while their budgeting template reveals payment of $435 for a car repair, there is no mention of it here, because even though they had a financial buffer account, they did not need it, simply because they had enough money in their discretionary expenditure account to cover them.

Also, in October we see the Ricardo's have a sudden once off expenditure of $2700 for a sudden medical bill. Now this kind of one off expense does come along every now and again. In the log we see that they covered $500 from their discretionary expenditure, however, the other $2,200 came from the financial buffer fund! How do you think they would have coped if they had not got this money set aside?

Well the good old credit card of course! And that's the whole point of the financial buffer fund, More often than not often than not it will keep things moving along , without falling right back into the debt trap all over again!

And do remember, that it's not about having a financial buffer which can insulate your debt reduction efforts from everything, under the Sun. Rather it's about having enough money set aside, so as to make sure that you if something comes out of the blue, once in a while, that you have a fair chance of managing to keep the debt reduction process on track, rather than having to dip into your credit cards, in an effort to look for a 'get out of jail card'.

Maintain the Financial Buffer Account Even After You Have Become Debt Free

Another consideration is that, even when you have become debt free, do maintain this account. As a matter of fact, unless you become really well off and have lots of excess money to spare, I strongly recommend that you maintain this financial buffer account. Of course, once you become debt free you no longer have to worry about maintaining a debt reduction process.

However, as mentioned in the other pillars of credit card debt freedom, it's not just about debt reduction, it's equally important to maintain the state of being debt free, and one of the single best ways to achieve this is to set aside an amount which is designed to cover sudden expenses!

Finally, it must be reiterated that the financial buffer account is a great tool, which will prevent backsliding into credit card debt. I know it's very easy to think that maybe maintaining a bank account with as much as $2500 in it is a waste of money, but do remember that it prevents backsliding.

Take the sample financial buffer account template above, with the examples of the Ricardo's; over the course of the year they have to dip into the account twice. The first time is to cover the expenses of a wedding, the second time they had to cover a sudden emergency with a medical emergency which costs them nearly $3,000!

The idea behind the financial buffer fund is not to protect the debtor from everything under the Sun, but it will help them to keep things on track, without resorting to the credit card. In the case of the Ricardo's only twice a year did they need to dip into the fund, but this is how one would expect it to be. If a debtor has to dip into the fund every month, then there is something out of kilter with their budgeting in the first place!

It's important to realize that the financial buffer fund, can only work, as long as the debtor has enough money free to make ends meet in the first place.

We will return to this theme later, but basically whatever debt relief option which you decide to follow, whether it be budgeting, debt consolidation, debt settlement or even bankruptcy, you must be able to make ends meet, throughout the entire process. If you cannot make ends meet, it indicates that you are following the wrong course of action, and need to make some changes!

Getting back to the validity of the financial buffer fund, it can seem like a waste of money to deposit some cash into this account, each and every month, when often you will not have to dip into it for many months. However, as noted, most of us will have a few sudden one off expenses which come out of the blue.

So, in reality, you will have to cover the expense anyway. Which means that rather than waiting for the sudden expenses, to come along and trying to figure out what to do when the expense came around, by depositing a small amount of money into the fund each and every month, until the fund reached a respectable level, it simply diverts some of your money onto a special account which can be used to deal with these one of expenses.

For example, in the case of the Ricardo's they managed to cover a wedding, while only withdrawing $220 form their financial buffer account, however, they nearly emptied the buffer account out completely in order to cover a medical emergency! Also, more than likely, without the financial buffer account, the bill of $2,700 would have gone onto their credit cards, and rebooted the credit card debt spiral in the process!

Also, to address any concerns, which you may have, about holding so much money in an account, rather than using it to clear of debt, two things need to be pointed out.

First off, regarding cash flow, if you take that money and use it to pay of your debts and then suddenly have to pay out on a large medical expense, such as a medical emergency, where will you get the $2700? Well your credit card of course, and you cannot call up your credit card company and ask them to reimburse the money which you have paid them over the last few months, now can you?

Secondly, there are quite a few bank accounts, which will deliver interest, and yet are flexible enough to allow several withdrawals year. Consequently, if you decide to open a financial buffer account, and are considering an interest account, do make sure to pick an account which allows for at least several withdrawals a year.

This means that if you put money, into this account, and begin the year with a balance which is equivalent to two months' worth of minimum payments, and you finish with that amount, it will bring about some interest, whereas if you did not have the account, you will receive no interest at all!

As a final consideration, if your finances are so out of kilter that you have thousands of dollars, in monthly minimum payments, and only a small amount of money which can be set aside, towards paying of debt, then maybe you need to tidy up your finances, a little bit, prior to setting up a buffer account.

By way of illustration let's take two debtors:

Debtor A has a disposable income of $2,000 a month, after general expenses, which they can spend on debt repayment, and yet they have a total of $1,000 a month to make on minimum payments, while at the same time owing $50,000. This means, that they can spare $1,000 a month, towards paying back that $50,000 in outstanding debt.

Now I would recommend, to this person, to set aside $2,000 (two months minimum payments) into a financial buffer account, so that even if some sudden expense comes up, that they will be able to at least make minimum payments, on any given month, and thus avoid the re-accrual of credit card debt!

Remember, at a debt of $50,000, that even if they were to instantly start setting aside an extra $1,000 a month, it will still take several years to clear the debt. In order to maintain progress with the repayment plan, it makes sense to set aside a couple of thousand dollars into a financial buffer fund. After all, if they don't touch the money, it will accrue interest, and if they have to touch the account, at least, it is better to withdraw money from a flexible savings account, rather than letting our credit cards take the hit instead!

However, let's take a look at Debtor B, who also owes $50,000 in debt and whose monthly minimum payments are $1,000 a month. However, they only have an expendable income of $1,000 a month, after all general expenses. Now the best that they can hope for is to make minimum payments, and as noted earlier, minimum payments will take around seven years (or possibly longer), to clear, and that's only as long as they make no new credit card purchases along the way.

Now in this case, it would be absurd for them to set aside two months minimum payments into a financial buffer fund, simply because by so doing so they would end up missing their minimum payments, for those two months, which would of course incur even more debt! And more importantly still, it's crazy to clear debt by paying off minimum payments alone!

So let's reiterate this:

It's Crazy to Clear off Debt, by Paying Minimum Payments on Credit Card Debts!

In the case of credit card debtor B, they should make a point of reducing their minimum payments, via either negotiation, as in credit card reduction or via credit card debt settlement!

So while in general, it's a good idea to create a financial buffer fund, the basics have to be right, from the get go. My recommendation to you is to read through this entire book and prune expenses and debt repayments, as necessary, and make sure that once you initiate a debt repayment plan, that it is realistically doable, without requiring any draconian measures on your part. Even if it takes a long time, to achieve a state of debt clearance, it's the slow but sure route, which will work in the majority of cases!

The Road to Debt Freedom is Littered with the Dead Bodies of Financially Faulty Ideas!

We all have to face up to facts now and again, and the simple reality behind becoming debt free, relies upon the letting go of all sorts of fallacious financial ideas. If the points raised in this article sound absurd to you, then it's time to challenge your financial concepts, because while setting aside some money, so as to keep the debt reduction process on track, may seem overboard, however, it is a simple necessity of life to make good financial decisions. And quite simply for most individuals, unless they have bundles of excess money, available to them, it just makes good financial sense to keep some money aside for a rainy day!

So do you and your debt reduction process a favour, and set some money aside for a rainy day. If two months debt repayments sound like too much, then simply reduce it to one month's debt repayments which you set aside!

Remember, it's not about the amount of money, rather it's about the concept of setting some money aside for a rainy day. During the debt reduction process, it is necessary to provide yourself with a financial buffer, in case of a sudden financial setback. However, even when you get yourself debt free, it's simply a good idea to keep some money aside, by way as a 'get out of jail card'. Put it this way, it is better to keep your 'get out of jail card' as a bank deposit account, rather than as the credit balance in your credit card!

I will mention idea repeatedly, in the 5 pillars to credit freedom program, that most debt problems arise out of a lack of understanding, regarding financial realities. And when we are unprepared, or are badly prepared, to deal with reality, then we end up reacting by going into debt!

By keeping some money aside for a rainy day, it not only aids the debt reduction process, but also it helps to keep you debt free, because you are responding rather than reacting to real life situations!

Now, that we have got you some debt reduction protection, the next stage in the process of getting yourself debt free, is to set some goals, which will help to keep you on track with the debt reduction process!

Chapter Five - The Fourth Key to Debt Freedom – Effective Financial Planning

A plan to set up some new financial goals, so as to help you become debt free, rather than focusing on endlessly putting out fires in your finances

Everything else, which we have covered so far, in the 5 pillars to credit card debt freedom, will bring you what you need, in order to become debt free. By abstaining from accruing new credit card debt, by budgeting in an effort to drive more money into the debt reduction process, and by placing some money into a special account, in order to buffer yourself and your family against any sudden financial setbacks; all these tactics will all help to keep the debt reduction process moving forward.

While these factors will help to make you debt free, the fourth pillar, whereby you set new financial goals, will help you to remain debt free, which is equally important!

There are four mistakes which most credit card debtors make, when attempting to become debt free, and they are the following:

- Relying too heavily upon will power rather than motivation
- Denial
- Societal pressure
- Debt cycle repayment structure

All of these factors have been covered in detail, in the earlier sections. In brief summary, the debt repayment cycle is designed to keep you in debt, and societal pressures combined with denial of your precarious financial situation, add up to a toxic cocktail which helps to maintain your indebted state.

By following the tactics laid down so far, in the pillars of credit card debt freedom, you can become debt free quite quickly.

But it also must be remembered, that becoming debt free is only half of the process; a great many credit card debtors manage to get this far only, to fall back again into poor financial habits. By setting new financial goals, it will become possible to motivate yourself towards something better, which is the single best way to ensure that you remain debt free forever!

Why Setting Financial Goals is so Necessary

if You Want to Remain Debt Free!

In life motivation is everything!

If we look back at the earlier sections, we noted how it is societal pressures, combined with the debt cycle repayment structure, and the tendency in human begins to be in denial about their financial situation, which all leads back into the credit card debt cycle. The mistake which many credit card debtors make, is in thinking that their financial situation is purely situational, a mere result of some bad luck combined, perhaps with some bad financial decisions.

While on the face of it, your financial situation may appear this way, in reality if it were purely situational, then surely a little bit of belt tightening and common sense would have brought you into the debt Free State long ago! However, while this might be the case for a small number of credit card debtors, in the majority of cases, the debt is a reoccurring problem. For many credit card debtors, they manage to reduce the debt only to find themselves right back in it once again. This may very well be the situation with you, in which case you can comfort yourself by realizing that you are not alone!

While the technical factors, such as the insipient nature of the credit card debt cycle, combined with the endless societal pressures, do have an effect, at the end of the day your financial situation is your responsibility. Because many people, manage not to get into credit card debt in the first place, and surely if they can keep debt free so can you!

So the question then, which lies behind your financial situation, which you need to ask yourself is as follows:

"Why did I get into debt in the first place?"

Forget about excuses, and forget about your circumstances and think instead about your mind-set. Ultimately, if you have found yourself getting mired into debt, and that even when you managed to become debt free in the past, only to find that pretty soon, you were back into debt all over again, then the real reason behind your credit card debts, has to lie with you and whatever is driving you to make your financial decisions. Societal pressures, the wicked credit card companies, and their credit card debt cycle are all simply outer aspects of your problem.

If you keep finding yourself returning to an indebted state, then you have been living in a state of financial denial, and you have to ask yourself why?

The why behind denial is ultimately about anxiety, and the impulsive need to relieve oneself temporarily from this inner state of stress!

Behind any repetitive financial problem, which is preventing you from staying debt free, there is always negative thinking, which has you feeling stressed, and which results in denial of your financial situation and general life status.

The real reason why most debt reduction processes fail is not due to technical issues or poor income or situational factors at all. The real reason, why you and most credit card debtors, fail to remain debt free is because of negative thinking and a belief that by applying ones willpower, that you can become debt free. In reality willpower is just like applying the gas pedal in your car. As long as you keep your foot on the gas, the car moves forward, however, as soon as you remove your foot, the car grounds to a halt.

By the same token, when we feel rattled by our debts, and we apply our willpower, it works for a little while, but then all too soon, our willpower wanes and behind all the outward activity the negative thinking patterns remains. Within no time at all, you find yourself becoming stressed, a little bit of denial sets in and before you know what happened, you are right back into debt again!

So changing our thinking patterns is really important if we want to become debt free, and remain in this state. However, changing thoughts is a difficult and time consuming process.

There are many great books out there which cover the subject of positive thinking and positive beliefs in a thorough fashion, so I recommend that you get reading. However this process is time consuming, because you have to change so many financial beliefs and habits.

However, a very simply thing which you can do today, which will help you to get debt free and remain debt free, is simply to set some positive financial goals. Because while changing financial thinking patterns and life beliefs might take a few years, to master properly, you can motivate yourself in less than five minutes, via the proper application of financial goals!

How to Set Financial Goals

Which are Meaningful to You!

If you are interested, in becoming debt free, and you want to set some financial goals to help with the motivation, then the most important factor is relevancy. The financial goals have to be meaningful, if you want them to inspire you. As noted earlier, most credit card debt is initiated because of denial which comes about as a way of defending ourselves against anxiety.

While the long-term cure is to increase self-esteem via positive thinking, setting inspirational financial goals is an instantaneous way of hotwiring the positive thinking process, because even though we may suffer from a lack of positive thinking and positive uplifting beliefs, we can all be ignited by desire!

Just take a look at how many people buy lottery tickets! They might have no money and a bundle of debts, but they still feel inspired to buy a lottery ticket, because their desire is leading them!

So that's the theory anyway, but we have to manifest this in the real World, which means that if you want to set financial goals which will inspire you towards achieving something with your life, then they need to be meaningful to you.

How Do You Make Financial Goals Meaningful?

This requires two things, which are:

- The financial goal has to believable:
- It has to be something which you feel you could achieve in the real World.

The financial goal has to be doable:

It has to be something which you can see yourself doing, once again in the real World.

The reason why so many self-help books and programs fail to deliver success is because they set outlandish goals, which their participants do not believe are either possible or doable!

So, while we all might like to get excited, every now and again; for a financial goal to work for us in the real World, it has to be inspirational, and to be inspirational you have to believe it is possible and doable!

So, for example, if you set the financial goal of becoming a millionaire by end of the year, you may feel excited, but you probably will not feel it to be a very believable goal. Whereas, if you take a look at your circumstances and decide on something which you would like to achieve, say taking your family on a holiday, without using a credit card to pay for the trip, and then set this as a goal, it is more likely to really inspire you!

Financial goals have to be believable and doable, if they are to be of any inspirational use to you!

Also, your financial goals have to appeal to you rather than someone else. So for example, many debtors would find the image of relaxing on a beach with nothing to do as an inspirational goal, however, if this does not excite you then don't opt for it.

Financial goals have to be meaningful, to you personally, so you must opt for financial goals which excite your interest, rather than someone else's. So maybe you like to travel rather, than hang out at the beach, in this case create a financial goal with reflects this aspiration!

Creating Financial Goals does

Not Have to be a Chore!

So if you want, to become debt free, set some financial goals which are believable, doable and of interest to you!

How to go about creating financial goals?

This does not have to be a chore, but it can be a little bit difficult to come up with inspirational goals, simply because most of us are so overwhelmed, by external stimuli, that we have forgotten to look inside ourselves for inspiration!

So, first things first, just forget about what you have seen on TV, or whatever it is that's being marketed at you. The generic goals, of great wealth and life on some serene beach, is a really compelling image, which is why it's so popular, but this does not mean that you would like to end up living on a beach, now does it!

This beautiful image appeals because it's a dreamy image, combined with the fact that most of us have spent a few nice days out at a beach, at some time, in the course of our life. However, when we are thinking of financial goals, we have to be a little bit more realistic and grounded in our approach. For a start we obviously want to become debt free, but what else do we want, what else do you really want to do with your life?

Start thinking in terms of interests and long held aspirations. If you are part of a family unit, start thinking about the aspirations of your various family members, and see how they fit together. It's important at this stage, in the financial goal setting process, to apply what's commonly referred to as 'blue sky thinking', which means that you don't let reality get in the way, rather you simply open your mind to the possibilities.

At this stage, in the financial goals setting process, simply throw ideas around and talk out loud with various family members and friends and try to get a feel for what would rock your boat!

If anybody gives you a hard time, telling you that it's important to get debt free first, simply concur with them, but remind them that it's necessary to aim for something meaningful with your life, and that you are looking for some sort of direction. This will usually get most quarrellers to agree with you, at least in principle!

So, once you have a few basic ideas about what excites you and your family, start to come back down to Earth and think in terms of timeframes, and start getting a little bit more practical.

For example, you may come to the conclusion that you can become completely debt free in two years, if you are sensible. In this case you can also think in terms of a life goal which you would like to achieve, if you were debt free, but which you are held back from achieving because of your outstanding debts.

Say, by way of an example, you may like the idea of going on a Para- gliding holiday every year, but you cannot make this a reality until you are debt free. Well now you have your first tangible goal which you will fulfil, as soon as you become debt free!

Short term goals also help with the process, of becoming debt free. If we think about it, keeping our nose clean with little or no excitement over a two year period is very difficult, so some short term financial goals can also be set to help inspire the process!

Maybe, if you are an outdoor person, you can give yourself a pat on the back, by taking a mini-break once you reach the halfway mark, and set aside a little bit of money for that. Or maybe you would like to do some traveling, so you take a weekend break with your family at certain strategic milestones, during the process of becoming debt free!

Why Financial Goals can be Leisure Goals

These goals, which I have mentioned here, apparently have nothing to do with financial goals; however nothing is further from the truth. To become debt free, it is necessary to have the basic financial goal of becoming debt free, and ideally to aim for enrichment in personal finances is another good medium to long term goal, so as to make for a wealthier future.

However, it must be remembered that while these points are true, it is also true to say that the debt reduction process can be a gruelling one, which is filled with personal self-sacrifice, and as such if it becomes too gruelling for the debtor, it is quite likely that they may give up on the debt reduction process and end up relapsing into credit card debt all over again!

So there is definitely a place in setting financial goals, for leisure based goals, and they can be classified in two different ways:

- Short–term goals - that are a pat on the back.
- Medium-term goals - that inspire you to focus on becoming debt free.

So, if we take the example of a debtor who reckons they can become debt free in two years, the medium term goal will be something to inspire them to become debt free. The way to think about it is in terms of monthly outgoings, so if a debtor is spending $1,000 on the debt reduction process, then they may think in terms of what they could achieve with their life, once the debt is repaid, and this money is diverted into something more useful.

Now if we suppose that half of this money be diverted into long term financial wellbeing, this still leaves $500 free for some sort of leisure activity. So focusing upon what you and your family can do with the money, which you save once you are debt free, this is a really great medium term goal to aim for.

For a couple, who would like to go on a Para-gliding holiday every year, for instance, then once they clear their debts, perhaps they can divert half of the money, which is now available, since the debt is cleared, so that they can go on such a holiday every year, while the other half can go towards long-term acquisition of wealth. Such a tactic is a very good way of using medium range goals, to pave the way towards long-term goals.

Because the new found paragliding holiday, when combined with an increasing rather than reducing bank account balance, is a great way to help the one time debtor to become really excited about becoming wealthy, because they can see the process working in real time. It's no longer a case of imaginary thinking rather they are beginning to create the life for themselves, which they have always dreamed off!

Also, once again, looking at the debtor who has a two year repayment schedule, it has to be remembered that two years may be a short time in the comparison with a life time, but it is still a long time when you are living it! So once again setting an affordable leisure goal, at a certain milestone, is a good way to pat you on the back.

Maybe, a good short-term goal would be to spend $500 on some family outing every time you achieve another milestone, such as paying off another 25% from the outstanding debt, for instance. It is worth this small expenditure, because it inspires you to continue on the road towards becoming debt free.

So, in an ideal World our financial goals may be purely economic in nature, however we must remember that for most of us, financial goals are really only there so that we can have the money set aside to do the things which we want to do. More than likely, you got yourself into debt, because of some activity which resulted out of the denial of your financial situation, whereby you felt anxious and sought some kind of financial succor via credit cards and other forms of credit.

Furthermore, the World which we live in is filled with all sorts of desirable wants being thrown in our faces. So, by providing some degree of leisure goals, it is good if at the end of the day, it brings us to a state whereby we have become debt free!

Becoming Debt Free and Remaining Debt Free by Setting and Fulfilling Financial Goals

By setting and fulfilling these basic financial goals, whereby you provide yourself and your family with some kind of leisure orientated perks once you achieve some degree of freedom from debt, this will help to inspire you to become debt free, which is really great.

However, this is simply the beginning, remember that most credit card debtors find themselves in debt because of a denial of their basic financial reality, whereby they attempt to comfort themselves and fit into society by spending today and paying back tomorrow.

However, once you get your financial goals set up right, and are willing to do whatever it takes to keep with the debt relief program, another possible reality opens up for you and your family, whereby you can actually create the lifestyle which you always wanted without getting into credit card debt, personal loans, overdrafts and all the other nonsense which is pushed down our throats by society today!

By applying the lessons learned, in the various sections of the 5 pillars to credit are debt freedom, it will be possible for you to work out just how much money you need to make ends meet each month and then to work out what you really want from your life, and set aside the money to achieve this financial goal.

So, for example, the debtor who is paying out $1,000 a month on a debt reduction program has to pay back the money which they owe plus the interest. However, this debt more than likely accrued due to the debtor being in a state of denial of their financial situation; by taking the steps outline in the 5 pillars, they will find themselves learning not only how to become debt free, but also how to set aside money for the future.

If you owe money today, once it is paid off you will have that much extra money available to spend where you like. Also if you get used to budgeting, you can learn how to save money and redirect it elsewhere.

The real key here is to learn how to live on less today and then to redirect this money into things which you really want in the medium to long-term. So, with the example of a debtor which is paying back $1,000 a month, they may find that in the process of following the debt reduction process that they have managed to reduce their expenditure by $500 a month, so that once the debt is repaid, they will have that $1,000 a month free to redirect elsewhere, plus they may also have another $500 available because they learned how to live on less.

Now if they are sensible they might direct $750 a month into long term financial security, but they can also redirect the other $750 a month into leisure activities.

Now here is the vital aspect of this process. If you can re-educate yourself to live on less today, as long as the rest of the money is set aside to a better tomorrow then two things become possible:

Firstly:

You can redirect some money to medium and long-term financial goals, whereby you cover such things as pensions, educational funds for your kids, as well as maintaining a financial buffer account, to protect your family from a rainy day. So, by becoming really sensible, you can have the financial buffers in place which help to prevent you from ever having to reach for a credit card or line of credit ever again.

Secondly:

Rather than spending indiscriminately, on silly purchases every day, if you get used to setting some money aside for things which you really want, and aligning these things which your life goals, it becomes possible to redirect this extra money in order to fulfil leisure goals, on things and activities which you really like, and this in itself will help to keep you debt free!

Let's put it this way, the society in which we live paints all sorts of pretty pictures of happy people carrying out all sorts of leisure actives. However, for most of us, who are living on a limited budget, it is not viable to live like that.

So what do we do?

Well, most of us give into the temptation to have the things today, which we cannot really afford, in the hope of paying them off tomorrow, when our financial situation is a little better. However, our financial situation rarely gets better, or if it does it still never quite manages to keep up with our ever expanding range of wants!

Now to burst a bubble, if you want to become debt free and remain debt free, then it is absolutely essential that you get real about your financial situation and start living within your means. Because there is absolutely no end to the TV adverts, and all the other forms of media, suggesting that you spend your money on one thing or another. However, this does not mean that you have to live like a pauper!

Things might be a little bit difficult for you and your family today, but don't focus on that, rather focus upon getting out of debt and learning and applying the lessons which are in the 5 pillars to credit card freedom.

Because, while you cannot live a millionaire lifestyle, on a small or medium income level, you can learn to have many of the good things in life if you have your head screwed on the right way!

By taking the time out to see what you really want in life and then cutting out wasteful expenditure, according to your financial situation, it will become possible to live a far more fulfilling life than you would ever have thought possible.

For example, the debtor who becomes debt free and finds themselves with $750 free a month, after covering all outgoings and keeping some money aside for their families long term financial wellbeing, if they redirect that $750 meaningfully they can have a surprisingly nice lifestyle. In the case of $750 a month, it adds up to $9,000 a year.

Now $9,000 a year, if spent appropriately, will make for a nice lifestyle if it is spent on only a few things. For example, maybe a family vacation and some money spent on your favourite hobby. However, if you do what most people do, which is to spend money left right and centre on all sorts of silly nonsense, this leisure fund will go nowhere!

So, I know we all like to be able to spend money willy-nilly, but as long as you are living on limited means, it makes more sense to set some money aside and spend it on a few well-chosen hobbies and leisure activities/products/services, rather than blowing your money with nothing to see for it at the end of the day!

Finally, the interesting thing which happens, when you set financial goals, is not only do you become debt free, but also you can learn how to live a life which you like to live. Because as you are living a life, which you do not like, the temptation to comfort spend will always be there. So, by setting financial goals and learning to live within a budget, this helps you to become debt free and once debt free you can start living a nice lifestyle, and more importantly a debt free lifestyle!

By finding out what it is that really makes life meaningful, to you and your family, and then aligning it with the compromises, necessary to set financial goals which match your income, it becomes possible to make leisure purchases which match your value system and which will deliver a nice lifestyle for you and your family.

Integrating Financial Goal Setting into Your Life

Ok, so much for the theory, so how do we go about making goal setting work for us in practice?

Just as we have noted down, in the second and third pillar, it is far easier to write things down rather than to carry them in our head. Have you ever noticed, for example, that it is really difficult to remember a phone number?

The reason is that most people can remember up to 5 numbers at one time, but few people can remember more than that. Obviously this was not a problem for our ancestors, who lived very simply lives, however, in the present day and age, where life is becoming increasingly complex and most of us have a thousand and one things on our minds? It can be really difficult to even gain an adequate understanding of a problem, let alone come up with a workable solution!

So what follows are a series of exercises which will help you define your financial goals and also monitor their progress. We will use the example of the Ricardo's once again, however, under the resources section there are links to the actual templates which you can use for your particular situation.

Blue Sky Thinking

So the best way to begin goal setting is to deploy some blue sky thinking. Just forget about all the limitations, for a minute, and instead shift your attention to new possibilities. Don't stop and say to yourself any of the following:

"I can't"

"I won't"

"We could never have enough money to do that!"

"I would love that, but we would never manage to do it!"

"It's unrealistic!"

"Just how do you plan to do that?"

"Stop dreaming!"

I know. It may be difficult to let go of all the negatives, however, at this stage your aim is to establish what you do want, rather than what is doable. Let's take a quick look at the Ricardo's first effort:

In order to gain a deeper insight, let's start by fleshing out our imaginary credit card debtors; let's take a quick look at their profile:

Profile:

Categories	Stakeholder 1(4)	Stakeholder 2
Names	John	Verona
Age	37	34
Education	BA	BCom, CPA
Occupation	Pharmaceutical Executive	hospital Administrative Assistant
Years in this career	11	7
Kids	2 (ages 11 and 8)	2 (ages 11 and 8)
Likes	The open, wild life and adventure	Excitement and change
Dislikes	Dislikes paperwork	Being hemmed in and office politics
Achievements	High School Athletics State Champion!	Travelled through six South American Countries on my own after graduating from college
Failures	Career still not progressing to manager level after 11 years in his career!	Decided to stay in US by turning down an Option to do an internship in Europe, not even married at the time, why miss Such an opportunity!

Now that we have some idea, as to what sort of people the Ricardo's are, and where they are coming from, now let's take a look at their long-term financial goals.

Blue Sky Thinking Financial Planning – Initial Overview: 01/10/2013

Categories	Stakeholder 1(4)	Stakeholder 2
Names	John	Verona
Age	37	34
Education	BA	BCom, CPA
Occupation	Pharmaceutical Executive	hospital Administrative Assistant
Years in this career	11	7
Kids	2 (ages 11 and 8)	2 (ages 11 and 8)
Likes	The open, wild life and adventure	Excitement and change
Dislikes	Dislikes paperwork	Being hemmed in and office politics
Achievements	High School Athletics State Champion!	Travelled through six South American Countries on my own after graduating from college
Failures	Career still not progressing to manager level after 11 years in his career!	Decided to stay in US by turning down an Option to do an internship in Europe, not even married at the time, why miss Such an opportunity!

Ok, so this is blue sky thinking, in action!

While in general the Ricardo's are quite down to Earth, both partners have some grand aspirations which may or may not be possible. For example, Verona's desire to travel by land and Sea across Europe and Africa, over the period of a year, may be a little bit impractical or certainly impractical until the kids have grown up! John's aspiration to generate great wealth, within a short time frame, maybe a little bit off the mark too.

However, while it is clear that everything cannot be achieved, some things are quite achievable. If we take a look at the list above, we can see that both John and Verona begin with fairly practical aspirations and then get into the swing of things towards, the end of the exercise, at which stage they start speaking about their hearts desire!

But here's the thing, this exercise is not about practicality, rather it's about reaching out and finding out what matters to you, what is your heart's desire.

Personally, I am not an advocate of the belief that you can have anything which you want, simply because you want it. I reckon that life does have certain limitations, and while it is very easy to suggest that a person can have everything which they want, it has been my personal experience that it is impossible to fulfil all of your wants.

However, there are two important factors to consider:

- While we cannot fulfil all of our wants, we can fulfil quite a few!

- While we cannot fulfil all of our wants, we can always fulfil all of our needs. So let's take a look at both of these aspects in a little greater detail

Fulfilling all of our wants?

Ok, so nobody can have it all their own way, all of the time. For example, if I want to become a millionaire businessman, maybe my family life may have to take second place, to building a business empire, and also vice versa, if my family life is the centre of my existence, then maybe my business has to take second place. Now second place doesn't have to mean that it doesn't receive attention, it's just that we all have to make priorities with our lives. Ultimately we cannot focus, on everything, all at once. After all there are only 24 hours in a day, and we have to take out a considerable portion of this time, simply to eat food, take care of our bodily needs and sleep!

Where I feel a lot of self-help advice goes wrong, is in suggesting that we can have a lifestyle whereby all our wants are met. This fantasy is also backed up by the advertising industry which loves to promote an ideal life image, of wealth alongside sloth and yet surrounded by family values!

We have all seen those ads on TV, which suggest the you too can become a millionaire and lie out on the beech all day, surrounded by sexy members of the opposite sex, while of course implicitly being well looked after by a loving romantic partner and sharing all of these with some loving well-adjusted kids!

Of course this is a fantasy!

For example, if you are wealthy, while you may get a chance to lie out on the beach, you will probably also have a lot of financial commitments and responsibilities which come along with wealth, and a great deal of time will usually be required to look after them.

If you have a loving romantic partner, well good for you, but that relationship also takes a lot of time and energy, for it to prosper!

It's no good just falling in love and simply living in the bloom of this romance forever. Individuals change and circumstances affect them, if you want a happy married life, then it requires a lot of work to keep it on the boil, and of course the same can be said of parenthood.

If our want a good relationship with your kids you will have to work at it, on a daily basis. And of course, nobody lives in vacuum, we all have inner emotional needs and wants and relationships with other individuals, such as our family and friends, and different people have different challenges in their life's, such as emotional issues, physical issues and so on, which makes life complex and challenging most of the time!

So I am not suggesting that life has to be hard, but it certainly is rarely easy!

If you want to have a successful life, you have to work at it and that means all aspects of it. For example, there is no point in settling down with a nice sexy partner, and then working 18 hours a day in your business and wondering why a year later, the relationship is a little bit strained!

So this is where accepting that we cannot have all of our wants comes into play. You see every now and then I switch on the TV and watch some show where some uber-rich person reveals their collection of 200 classic cars, or their 17 houses or whatever. Ok, good for them, chances are that I will probably never have the opportunity to have so many possessions, because it requires a vast income to buy all of this stuff. But here is the interesting thing; there is no end to desire!

Do you think that the guy with 200 classic cars is satisfied with his collection?

Probably not! That's not to say he isn't happy, but he probably wishes that he could have another few classic cars, and that if he owned them, that his collection would be even greater. You see there is no end to desire, so somewhere along the way we have to draw a line in the sand and say, ok I will be satisfied with what I have.

So if you have a $100,000,000 fortune are your disposal, then maybe a 200 car collection is a possibility for you, but even still at some stage you will have to say enough. After all how many cars can you drive at one time?

One, of course!

And what about maintaining that huge car collection?

Yep it's a lot for work!

So whether you have enough money, to own 1 car or 200 cars, at some stage you will have to call it a day, and this is when we have to realize, that for our own happiness and wellbeing, that we cannot fulfil all of our wants, as there is an never-ending supply of wants, lying in wait for all of us!

So the first realization, has to be the acceptance of the fact that we cannot have all of our wants fulfilled, it's simply impossible!

That said, by prioritizing we can focus on fulfilling the wants which are most relevant to us. Back to our example of the rich guy, who owns a classic car collection, maybe his collection means everything to him. In which case great. But what if he also wants a good relationship with his wife and kids, and yet he spends all of his time looking after his car collection, and yet on one side he feels distraught at his suffering family life, yet he has looked after these cars over the last 20 years and is the president of two or three classic car clubs, and so feels obliged to commit so much time to this exercise?

Well in this case, maybe if he did a little bit of introspection, he would relinquish some of his classic car activities and focus a little more on his family instead!

Ok, chances are that most of us will never be in this position of having a 200 car classic car collection. However, it's a good example because it is so obvious that this guy should spend more time with his family than with his cars!

However, for most of us, our challenges will be a little bit different; for example if we take a look at John Ricardo, he loves hill walking and paragliding, and would really like to get back to hill walking, however he seems to lack the time to do it, because it requires a full day to go on a hill walk, and between work commitments and the need to spend time with his wife and kids, it is difficult to find the time.

Now he lists down his desire, to get back hillwalking, and yet he also lists down his desire to earn more money, to do a fastback MBA program and to enter into management. So needless to say, something has to give, and in reality considering where he and his wife are at, with young kids and debts, more than likely the 'want' to go hill walking will have to give way to the career and financial 'needs'.

So this is a clear example of prioritizing wants, and also it's the sort of realistic example which most people will come across in real life. So, obviously some wants have to give away to more important needs. While it may sound obvious to say this, sometimes, in everyday life we lose sight of the wood for the trees, and we attempt to achieve too many things at once.

Returning to this 'blue sky exercise', on the level of wants, it produces two useful results. First off, it can reveal where some of our convictions lie, so this way we can have a think about what is the best way to prioritize. In the case of a couple, it becomes necessary to look at each other's goals and then to be willing to compromise so that both parties receive a fair deal.

Secondly, by listing idealized goals, while we may have to concede that some goals may be unrealistic, at least we can find what it is that we really desire. Because, in the tumult of everyday life, it can be very easy to become so involved in everyday activities that we lose track of what it is that we really like to do!

We can batten down the hatches and get on with life. Forcing ourselves to work in jobs which we do not like, and basically act in a very responsible manner, while this can be a good thing to do, because often by acting responsibly we can progress in life, if in the process, we lose track of what we really like to do in life, life itself can turn into a very tedious experience!

So while it may not be possible to fulfil a life dream, somewhere along the way we need to integrate things which are really important to us. We see this in the example of Verona Ricardo, a lady who reveals both in her profile and in her wish list a strong motivation towards travel and adventure.

So while her idealized goal of traveling across Europe and Africa over the period of a year maybe be unrealistic, in the long term if she remains in an office job, with no excitement or travel, and does not do any traveling outside of work either, then she is ignoring a strong desire for travel and adventure!

So in her case maybe she will never go on a yearlong tour, however, for her long-term happiness, she needs to work towards satisfying her desire for travel, maybe not immediately but certainly once they resolve their debts, some changes need to be made!

Finally we can ask ourselves where this fits in with clearing our debts

It must be remembered, in this regard, that most of us drift into debt because we are living in denial of our life circumstances. Now, while this can relate to a lack of reality checking, whereby we simply live beyond our income, in which case we have to learn to live on less money, for the majority of people the debt can also arise out of a compulsive need to spend money in a comforting fashion, whereby they are attempting to plug holes in their life through their purchases!

Consequently, the reason for adding in a wish list, to the goal setting process, is to help ourselves to orientate towards a lifestyle which makes us happy. This will help to make us more content and so we will be more likely to keep away from comfort spending.

Also, once we have a clear idea as to what we want, we can work towards it because we can use the desire of pursing what we want as a motivational force!

Fulfilling all of our needs?

While it is clearly not possible to fulfil all of our wants, it is certainly possible to fulfil all of our needs. Actually our needs, are far fewer in number than our wants! Because it must be remembered that while wants are forever increasing, needs are quite finite in number!

The most obvious needs of course, are those of basic human survival, such as food, water, shelter and warmth. However, as we can see by looking over both the profile of the Ricardo's and their 'wish list', that there are certain things which keep coming up over and over again. Verona Ricardo, for instance, has a strong desire for freedom and travel, while John Verona has a strong desire to pursue outdoor activities; so these desires represents significant 'wants' for each of them. However, as we can see, by looking at their entries, the sheer repetition of these desires represents a need as well as a want!

If a desire keeps on repeating itself, over and over again, chances are that it's actually a need!

Obviously we are not living in the Stone Age! It is not enough to presume that our needs, are only physical, rather a significant number of our needs are internal rather than external, since as human beings we spend a significant amount if our time living within ourselves, so that we need to feel good about ourselves, and how we achieve this will vary from one person to another!

This means that while we cannot satisfy all of our wants, we can fulfil all of our needs, and furthermore, some of our wants are our needs!

While it is fair to say that, we are a losing track, if we pursue each and every one of our 'wants', some of our wants are in fact needs, and these need have be addressed!

By, way of an example, if a person has a strong inclination towards music say, throughout their life, they love listening to music and perhaps performing in some way then it is fair to say that music is a need for them.

If we look back at the adventurousness of John Ricardo, se see a man who needs some outward activity, and yet he spends most of his time in the office.

So it is fair to say that in his case he needs to integrate this 'need' of outward activity, into his life!

I cannot, emphasize this enough, that is the differentiation between needs and wants, because while we cannot fulfill all of our wants, some of our wants are in fact needs, and these needs reveal themselves though the medium of our wants!

The big thing is to do some soul searching and see what really matters to you. If it is only a want, then you will be able to get by without it, whereas a need which is unfulfilled will leave you feeling barren and withdrawn. And the key to progressing away from debt and towards wealth, is to develop a lifestyle which although perhaps a little austere, is yet bearable because you are on track to fulfill all of your needs, including the subtle inner mental emotional needs.

After all, eventually when you arrive at a state of financial security, the amount of wants can be allowed to be increased. But for now, it is necessary to reduce unnecessary expenditure, while keeping things on track.

Only ever sacrifice 'wants' and not 'needs'!

So the essential thing to do, at the initial stage, of the initial overview, is to discern what it is that you need, and what it is that you desire. Because once underway, with financial goal setting, some sacrifices will have to be made, and the only way to move forward is by setting priorities and making sure that you only sacrifice your wants and not your needs!

Needs, Wants and Dreams!

Ok, so now you have a fair idea about what you like, and what you need, and which wants are needs as well as wants. You have also managed to take a peek into what you really want out of life, by carrying out the blue sky thinking exercise!

Look at it this way, not only does the initial overview provide an insight into your desires versus your needs, but it also allows for the possibility of opening your mind and heart up to speaking out about what you would really like to do with your life. While in one way, this is deeply impractical and can firmly be placed under the heading of 'wishes' rather than 'needs', it must also be remembered that when following the 5 pillars, the initial efforts will require a certain level of self-sacrifice, whereby some of your wants will have to be repressed, however, in the long-term the plan is to increase your wealth to such a degree that once again some wants can be included in your daily lifestyle.

Take a quick look at the diagram below, which outlines the mix between wants, needs and fulfilment of life dreams:

Figure 4 - The Debtors Dilemma!

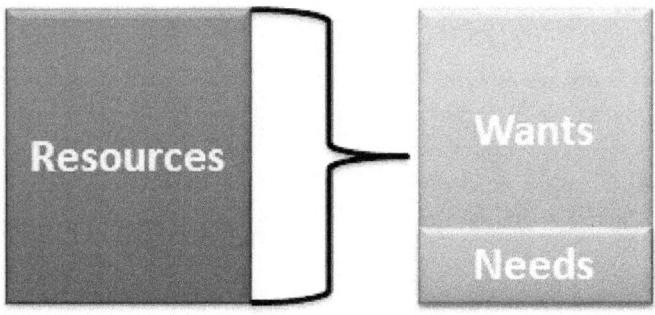

In this diagram we see the initial problem of the debtor, who has limited resources and a great many wants. Here, the wants are far greater than their resources. Yet we can clearly see that their needs are actually far smaller than their resources; if only they could cut out their wants and live within their needs, how quickly they could resolve their debt problem!

Of course, as noted in the last section, some apparent wants are also needs, so it's a subtle subject. Basically, in order to get our finances in order we have to restrict our outgoings, but not so much so that we completely stifle ourselves, which would end up making the debt reduction/wealth progression process an unbearable one!

It's ok to fulfil 'wants' as long as the debt reduction/ wealth progression program is still on track!

By way of example, if we take a look again at the Ricardo's, while sorting out their debts, it is clearly obvious that going on worldwide trips and living the outdoor life is a no-no! However, they can still make an effort to carry out some of the activities which they love, such as some traveling and outdoor activities, as long as they keep within their budget!

In the next figure, we see the progress from wants and needs to pursuing dreams. This is really a snapshot of where the debtor can be once they clear off their debts and begin progressing upwards towards wealth. Ultimately we are not against 'wants', rather we have to realize that for a little while we must restrict our wants, and only reinstate them once we are well on the way to becoming debt free:

Figure 5. The Wealthy Persons Paradigm!

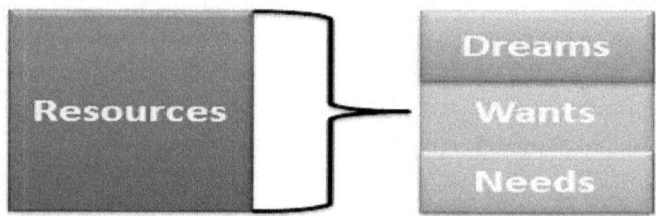

Interesting, with the wealthy person paradigm, we see no more resources however we see a re-arrangement of the boxes on the right. 'Wants' have been significantly reduced, 'needs' remain the same, and a new box, entitled 'dreams', is now in place.

So first off, the person in the wealthy paradigm, does not necessarily have to earn any more money than the indebted person, rather they simply have to be better at allocating resources!

Let's put it this way, an individual could be earning a big income, such as $300,000 a year, but if they spent $330,000 a year pursing endless 'wants' then they will quickly indebt themselves!

By the same token, another individual could be earning $15,000 a year, and yet if they only spend $10,000 a year, then they will actually be $5,000 richer at the end of the year, than the person who earned $300,000!

Initially, the debtor has to reduce their debts, and by reducing 'wants', this is the best way to achieve this. Finally, once the debt is cleared, the money which has been allocated towards debt clearance can now be relocated towards pursuing long-term goals, which we are categorizing here as dreams!

If we take a look at the Riccardo's, for instance, once free of debt, they will have an extra $26,144 a year which they can put towards their goals!

The acquisition of wealth is not rocket science; even if the increase in wealth is minimal, over the medium to long-term, incremental increases in savings turn into wealth!

Becoming wealthy is not half as difficult as you may have been lead to believe; rather becoming wealthy simply requires good financial habits applied over a reasonable period of time. Even if the increase in wealth is slight, over time it becomes a large figure!

By, way of an example, as to the power of exponential wealth accumulation, I have charted out how a relatively small increment, of only $1,000 a month, quickly ramps up at the rate of $3,000 per quarter until the person who is accumulating wealth has managed to go from a positive bank balance of zero dollars to $52,000 within 16 quarters, which is 4 years!

Now, I know that if you have been going through a lot of debt problems, then maybe 4 years to achieve a positive bank balance of $52,000 does not sound like a lot, but let's put it this way it's an awful lot better having a positive bank balance of $50,000 rather than having a debt of $50,000 !

While a $1,000 does, not seem like an awful lot of increment, for someone looking to become wealthy, over time, it quickly accumulates into a considerable sum of money. Also, for the sake of simplicity, this diagram does not figure the possibility of interest earned during this time frame.

In reality most people who are accumulating wealth, will be investing a fairly large chunk of money into investments which will result in comprehensive interest on their investments, and this is a cornerstone of wealth accumulation.

Debtors, find themselves with leverage working against them, because interest is basically killing them! In particular we see this to be very much the case with credit card debt, with its double digit interest rates. However, all we have to do is to turn the leverage on is head, so that we have interest working in our favour.

Just take a look at the graph below. Its shows a comparison between $10,000 deployed in three different ways, as follows:

$10,000 balance on a four year loan, paid off at $244.12 a month, resulting in a total of $11,718 in expenditure (figure 6 below).

Figure 6 - $10,000 Loan

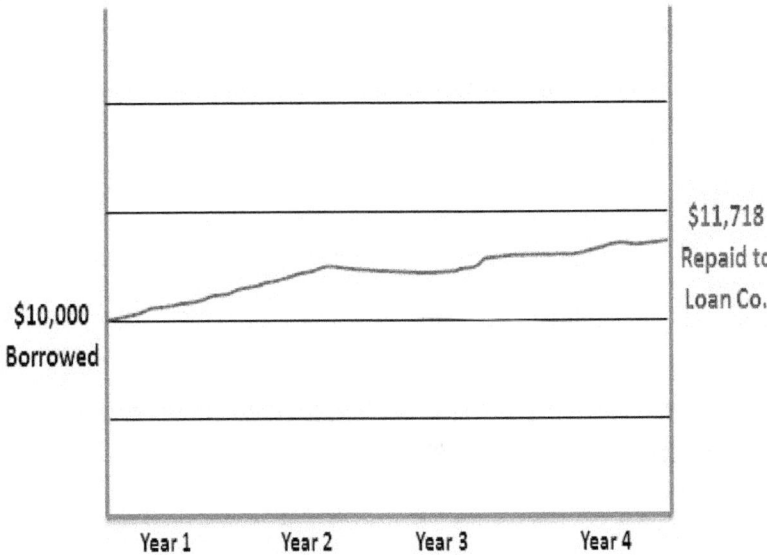

$10,000 balance on a credit card, paid off at $280 a month over a four year period, resulting in a total outlay of $13,330 (figure 7 below).

Figure 6 - $10,000 Credit Card Balance

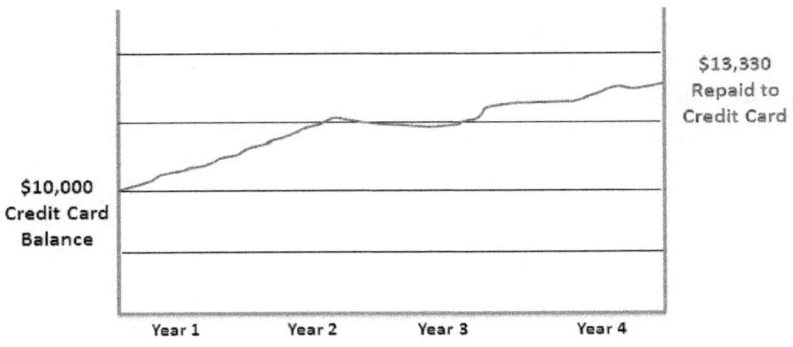

An initial investment of $10,000, with no additional installments, on a savings account, at the rate of 5% per annum, over the period of four years, resulting in a total savings of $12,155(figure 8 below).

Figure 7 - $10,000 Invested

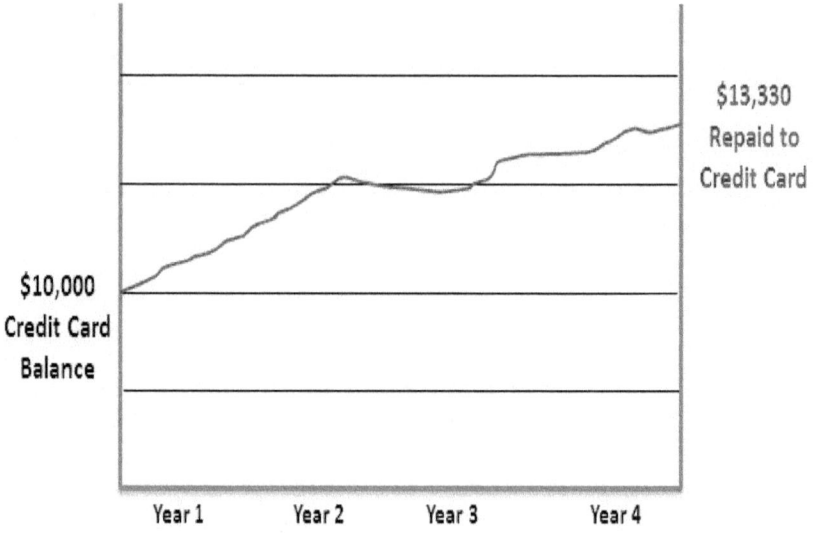

This graph is a simple way to illustrate how, even a relatively small amount, such as $10,000, delivers substantially different results, depending upon how it is leveraged. The regular loan, for instance, costs an extra $1,718, over the four years, while the credit card loan costs a whopping great $3,330 over four years!

Also , remember that this calculation is not based upon a debtor who is paying minimum payments, rather this is a debtor who is making a concerted effort to clear the credit card, as the industry average of 2% on the outstanding balance, would only equate to $200 a month, and would take over 7 years to clear. So if you have to take out a loan, take out a regular loan and not a credit card loan!

However, clearly when we compare this to the investor, who invests $10,000, even on a fairly conservative interest rate, such as 5%, that they leverage the interest, so that they have $2,155 in their back pocket at the end of four years, versus the credit card debtor, who has minus $3,330 out of pocket by the end of this period!

The Effect of Financial Leverage on Your Pocket, overtime. Choose debt and your money is leveraged downwards, choose investment and your money is leveraged upwards. Same initial balance, but different result!

We can see an enormous difference in wealth, and yet when it comes down to it, it's all about interest! So even though the investor has the lowest rate of interest, they end up in the best financial position at the end of three years, simply because their bank balance is constantly improving, rather than dis-improving over time!

Finally, while on one hand saving $1,000 may sound like a very small figure to some individuals, it may well sound like a colossal amount to others. So let's start this by stating that a lot of debtors, and debtors who have credit card debts in particular, are easily pouring out $1,000 or more per month on their minimum payments. So, I know that when we are in debt, it is difficult to even imagine possessing $1,000 at the end of the month, never mind saving $1,000! However, all it takes is for you to pay off your debts and then reinvest that amount of money in savings!

In order, to make the above example simple I have focused on a simple sum, such as $1,000. I know that for some people $1,000 is a small amount, while for others $1,000 is an enormous figure. However, like I have noted before, it's not about the money, rather it is about the continual application of good financial strategies, which over time, will first of all clear your debts, and then over another period of time, they will exponentially increase your wealth!

While it can be difficult to ascertain, exactly how much money you can save, over time, one thing is for sure, it will be at least equivalent to that amount of money, which you are presently spending each month on servicing your loans! While a lot of get rich quick books, and courses, suggest all sorts of amazing wealth increasing figures, at the end of the day, you are spending all of your disposable income on servicing your debts, so first things first, clear your debts and then invest your way into wealth.

For example, if you are presently pouring out $500 a month to service your loans, then at least you know that you can spend $500 a month! If spending $500 a month is getting you down, then think just how great you will feel by saving $500 a month! While it might sound amazing, it's all a case of perspective. $500 a month with interest on a loan is bad, $500 a month in investments with interest is good. Just get yourself over to the right side of the equation and you will do alright, believe me!

Keep on the right hand side of the equation and wealth will grow and grow!

To summarize, we all have needs and wants, and wants are always greater than needs! In fact, they tend to grow exponentially!

However, if we want to achieve anything with our life, we have to reduce some unnecessary wants, in order to make progress with our lives. Now, most people who have debt problems, have far too many wants, so much so in fact that they are pulling themselves apart trying to fulfil all of them at once!

So rather than tying ourselves in a knot, by carrying out the blue sky wish list exercise, we can see what is a wish and what is a need, because some needs appear to be wants, and some wants appear to be needs! Consequently, it requires a little bit of soul searching finding out what really matters to you. By reducing 'wants', and by fulfilling our needs (including those which appear like 'wants'), we can make progress, not only with reducing our debt mountain, but also with moving forward towards wealth generation!

Interestingly, when we take a look at figure 5, we see the benefits of reducing unnecessary wants, whereby we can actually start to pursue our dreams. This leads on quite nicely to the next stage in the wealth generation process, which is setting that timeline for goal achievement!

However before moving on to the timeline just think about this for a second, I made a point of elaborating the various types of wants and needs, and how the wish list exercise can help with this process, simply because it so vital. So many self-help books emphasize goal setting without ever raising the issue of just what goals need to be pursued, however, what a waste of time it would be to spend several years chasing after a goal which, when you achieved it, meant little or nothing to you!

While we are not going to go into depth regarding this subject of wish selection, as this would require an entire standalone book, just to cover this issue, it is enough to say that by taking the time out to fill in the profile and the wish list exercise, and do it several times if need be, until you feel quite comfortable with the results.

Maybe even consider taking a notebook and jotting down some notes about what you like, about what you dislike and about the various challenges which you have undergone in your life so far. Attempt to ditch any conditioned responses, such as 'I want to be rich", out of your system!

Rather this is about finding out what you really want with your life, and finding a way to create the space to move on with the process. Whether this takes you a day, a week or a month to achieve, when you feel that you have a fairly good idea about the sort of things which you would like to achieve in an ideal Word, and then move onto the timeline goal setting exercises below.

Creating a Goal Achievement Timeline

After carrying out this exercise, several times, you should have a fair idea about what you would like to achieve, in an ideal Word. Also it will provide you with a good idea, as to what you really need, versus what you really want. So now it's time to take a more in-depth look into what, it is exactly, that you would like to achieve, and what timeframe is necessary in order to achieve it.

First off let's start with the 'Silly want reduction' exercise. In this exercise we take a look at our 'blue sky thinking' and then we eliminate anything, however nice it may be, which can be classified as being a silly want, that is an unnecessary want, something which we may well like, but which we could easily live without!

Financial Planning – Silly Wish Reduction Exercise

Date: 07/10/2013 Real long –Term Goals

John Ricardo

1	To be free of all debts within two years		Doable
2	Take up fast track MBA program, once debts are cleared		Doable
3	Finally move into management once MBA is finished		Doable
4	Take kids on holiday to Europe; we have promised them that for the last four years!	Not Now, let's get out of debt first!	Doable, after we clear our debts!
5	Get back to hill walking (don't seem to have time these days!)	No time, once I go on the fast track MBA program	I can make a point of doing a few hill walks a year, but not consistently!
6	Save $1,000,000 (index linked) within 15 years!	Might be a pipe dream, as it requires around an average of $50,000 a year plus interest to achieve this!	Can save some money, probably 100k +, after kids funds etc., but unlikely to be $1 million dollars!
7	Have $100,000 in kid's college fund within 7 years!		Doable, as long as we invest around $10,000 a year plus interest
8	Become a millionaire in 10 years	Not going to happen, unless we win the lottery!!!!	
9	Own our own house in 10 years (and it has to be a big one, 2,000sq feet and in a nice location, ideally with a pool!)	Since we have only rented accommodation today, questionable. We could probably buy one, but probably not own it outright!	The house which we want would cost around $1,000,000, which even with a home loan might be a stretch. Possibly a nice house in the 500k range could be doable in that timeframe, unless we strike it lucky financially!

Verona Ricardo

1	To be free of all debts within two years		Doable
2	Consider career change once debts cleared, would like to set up some sort of travel business?		Doable
3	Take kids on holiday to Europe; we have promised them that for the last four years!		Doable, after we clear our debts!
4	Save $1,000,000 (index linked) within 15 years!		Can save some money, probably 100k +, after kids funds etc., but unlikely to be $1 million dollars!
5	Have $100,000 in kid's college fund within 7 years!		Doable as long as we invest around 10k a year plus interest
6	Travel by land and boat from Spain to South Africa over a period of a year, and write a book about the adventure!!!	Doable at some stage, but when? Probably have to wait for kids to be growing up first!	Maybe a doable goal in 10 years' time. In the meantime we can get going with holidays once debts paid off in two years!

While this exercise has a funny sounding name, it is a highly relevant title, because it allows the debtor to remove the wishes, which are simply impractical!

How? You might wonder why I am suggesting carrying out this exercise after the initial, 'wish list' exercise (quite probably anywhere from a week to a month afterword's)?

Basically, while you can perform the two exercises at once, most people will lack the clarity to really produce a sensible wish list to begin with. So we see in the example above, that the Ricardo's carry out this exercise a week after the first exercise, and that simply provides them with the opportunity to have a few attempts at this exercise.

Chances are, if you have not done this kind of thing before, that you might end up either staring at the page, unable to think of anything to put down, or you might end up writing an entirely useless list, whereby the entire list is filled with all sorts of nonsense, which you probably don't really want in the first place!

The challenge in these kinds of exercises is getting beyond the conditioning, so that we can actually find out, what exactly it is that we want out of life. As noted earlier, generic images of happiness by the pool might sell houses and cars, but often it turns out to be a shallow experience when we chase after such a goal.

In reality, we all have many wants and quite a few needs, and really it is necessary to find out what we really want in life, and then create a purposeful plan to get ourselves there. Finally, in the case of couples and families, there are often multiple wants and needs which have to be assessed; so really it takes quite a bit of soul searching to find out what route is the best one to take, not only for ourselves, but also for our families!

Both of these possibilities are fine, and really if this is the case with you, then it just goes to show how little most of us know about what we really want out of life! For most of us, we have been so bombarded by TV ads, newspapers ads and celebrity culture that we simply buy into the lottery ad image of lying by a swimming pool, surrounded by beautiful people! In reality, we are all far more complex than this, and quite simply what turns you on might be different from what turns somebody else on. It is pointless chasing after generic goals! You are an individual and you need to pursue your own goals!

By carrying out the 'silly wish list' exercise multiple times, a trend begins to reveal itself, and at last you will begin to gain clarity about what you really want, out of life. As noted earlier, it is necessary to give your mind free range, in this exercise, so that whatever is in your heart comes on out. If we take John Verona for example, if we ignore his silly wishes, then all that we will see is his interest in career success, while covering up his adventurous side. It is important for him to keep this side of his personality well nourished.

The 'Blue Sky Thinking' exercise brings to light, his adventurous side, while the 'Silly Wish List Reduction', exercise allows him to gain perspective, on what really matters now! In John Verona's case, he needs to focus presently on practical things, however, he needs to at least pay lip service to his adventurous side, and set longer term goals which take this aspect of his personality into account!

Of course, sacrifices do have to be made, looking once again at John Ricardo, in his 'Silly Wish List Reduction' exercise, he has more or less relegated his hill walking to a few days a year. While this may not sound good, at least he acknowledges this need, and is making a point of including it to a small degree.

However because his main focus is on career development and pursuing a fast track MBA program, once the debts are cleared, he will put this need for adventure, on the backburner, but not forever, just for around 3 years. While that sounds like a long time, at least he acknowledges this need and is moving towards it.

We see a similar take with Verona Ricardo's World travel plans, which are taking a 10 year delay! However even though both John and Verona Ricardo are making some sacrifices, at least they are accepting their needs, even if some of them have to be delayed for a while!

With the Ricardo's, their main priorities are getting out of debt, getting a college fund together for their kids and getting some kind of long term investment portfolio together, which will help them to become wealthy, in the medium to long-term. With this in mind, many of their needs will have to take a hit. But importantly, once we recognize a need, even if we have to delay it for a while, it frees up some internal energy. Rather, it's only when we are in denial of our needs, that we have a problem.

So, for example, if we want to get rid of our debts and then become wealthy, but are in denial of our needs, we will continually find ourselves becoming demotivated and slowly going of course, and that's because on an unconscious level we are holding ourselves back, because we are in denial of our needs!

We can deny wants indefinitely, however we can only put off needs for a limited period of time, otherwise our needs will literally tear us apart!

The key point to note here, is that while needs are limited and wants are unlimited, we can actually deny our wants indefinitely and still feel ok, once we get used to it, whereas we can only deny our needs for a limited time period, otherwise these needs will tear us apart!

In the case of the Ricardo's they are willing to put some needs on the back burner, but that does not means that they will not attend to those needs at a later point, rather they are just focusing on other priorities at the moment.

Also, another point to consider is the dismissal of some 'silly wishes'. For example, the desires to become millionaires, owning a huge house and possessing $1,000,000 in investments have been dismissed out of hand by the Ricardo's, why?

Because they are 'silly', as in they are not readily achievable. As it stands the Ricardo's are spending $2,177 a month, in servicing their loans. At their present rate of progress, they will be debt free in two years. If nothing changes then they will have $2,177 a month, which is $26,124 a year to invest in their dreams. Now what are their dreams? Well a college fund for their kids, money in the bank, a big house etc. Now this is where reality checking and prioritization come into effect.

Reality Checking

There is no point presuming that suddenly John Ricardo will get a huge pay rise, or that Verona Ricardo will have a hit business on her hands, so when setting goals it is better to presume that resources (that's income) stays roughly the same. I know that this goes counter to a lot of self-development, books and courses, which suggest that we can get rich overnight, simply by thinking about it, and that via the 'law of attraction' if we think ourselves rich, riches will suddenly arrive in our life!

To a degree, the law of attraction does work, however, personally I prefer to work with what I call 'the law of reality, which goes like this:

The Law of Reality

We cannot presume anything. Basically things tend to remain the same, unless we make some kind of radical change!

So if say John Ricardo is earning $55,200 a year, it is unlikely to change very much in the near future, unless something radical happens. Radical, could mean a demotion, or even loss of a job, or it could even mean a really big promotion or a new financial set up completely, such as a lottery win or an inheritance for example. However, more than likely his income will stay within a fairly narrow range, and will increase according to the strategic steps which he makes in his life.

So for instance, say John Ricardo spends some money on the fast track MBA program, maybe this will help him to make the jump into management, which he has being looking for, and suddenly he will be on $75,000 a year. Furthermore, if he asks around he might be able to ascertain that the average manager increase their earnings by maybe 50% over the next five year period, which brings his income up to around $110,000 a year within five years of becoming a manager.

Now naturally a lot of things can change, both positively and negatively in that timeframe, but more than likely if he is earning 55k a year today, he knows that once he becomes a manager, at least his income will jump to 75k immediately and usually hit the 100k+ figure within five years. Now what I like about this kind of planning is that although slow and conservative, it is predictable!

Whereas a lot of self-help books propose instant riches, simply by wishing it be so, they do nothing by way of creating a realistic game plan. Indeed, some self-help books even like to indulge in success stories about how somebody from humble beginnings suddenly received lots of opportunities thanks to positive thinking, the law of attraction or whatever. The annoying thing with this is that it's easy to enjoy reading about someone else's success. But does that mean that you will be a success, simply by wishing it!

Also, I have read lots of success stories which start by outlining the difficulties which a person had, and then suddenly skipping by a few years until we see the person arrive at a great success. To my mind this is like those murder mystery novels which hide the vital clues, so that it becomes impossible for the reader to solve the mystery, instead we have to wait for the investigator to reveal the clues (which were hidden form the reader) in the final scene of the book!

I'm not against success stories, however, rather I am against anything which simply sounds nice but which does not help the reader!

Back to reality checking; I am not against the law of attraction, and I feel that it's a really good idea to work towards great success in your life. However, behind all the self-help books, there are a huge number of distressed individuals who believed that they could be rich, who bought into this self-help course and who are still no better off today!

While there is a certain truth behind the law of attraction, I do not feel that simply believing you will get rich, is a good idea. It is better, in my opinion, to do a little reality checking and start to move forward with your life. At the same time, you can still believe that you will get rich and be open to it, however, in the meantime by moving forward with concrete plans, at least some progress is being made, and with each little bit of progress, it becomes possible to come a little bit nearer to the goal!

We see with john Ricardo, that while he might wish for great wealth, his income over the next 7 to 8 years will probably rise slowly from 55k a year, take a sudden surge forward when he finishes his MBA, and then grow fairly quickly to 100k+.

When considering these realities, it means that he can see that having a $1,000,000 in his bank account, plus $100,000 in his kids college fund, plus a $1,000,000 house, all in a fairly quick time period, is probably not going to happen. For example, Verona Ricardo will probably look for a career change once their finances improve, so let's say she opens a business, more than likely they will actually make less money for the first couple of years, while the business gets set up, and thereafter the business will probably only increase profitability quite slowly for the first few years.

This is the reason for prioritization. The biggest priority, for the Ricardo's, is clearing their debts, and the second biggest priority is taking the family on a European vacation, and the third biggest priority is taking care of their kids' college fund, because their kids will be finishing school in 7 and 10 years respectively. So again just taking a reality check, the Ricardo's are in their 30's, so even 10 years from now they will still only be in their 40's, so paying for their kids' college education is more important than having some kind of long-term investment/retirement fund.

What about the other priorities, well get the Ricardo's to fill in a quick prioritization list:

Timeframe	John Ricardo	Verona Ricardo	Priority List	Priority #
2 Years	To be free of all debts within two years	To be free of all debts within two years	Highest	1
3 Years	Take up fastback MBA program once debts are cleared		High	3
Anytime	Hillwalking		Low	9
7 Years	$100,000 college fund for the kids. Requires 10k a year investment	$100,000 college fund for the kids. Requires 10k a year investment	High	4
2 Years	Family holiday to Europe will require around $6,000. Also thereafter we want to set aside $3,000 for a family holiday each year!	Family holiday to Europe will require around $6,000. Also thereafter we want to set aside $3,000 for a family holiday each year!	Second Highest Priority	2
3 Years	Consider career change once debts cleared, would like to set up some sort of travel business?	Consider career change once debts cleared, would like to set up some sort of travel business?		5
15 Years	$1000,000 investment (not likely) for now first 7 years only we will be sending $10,000 on kids' college fund(plus it will need to be topped up in college] and $3,000 for holiday so conservative estimate of 26k-13k=13k for investment x 15 years =195k plus interest. So probably 300k in 15years! Hopefully increased income & good investments will boost it to the $1,000,000 k figure in 15 years!	$1000,000 investment (not likely) for now first 7 years only we will be sending $10,000 on kids' college fund] plus it will need to be topped up in college] and $3,000 for holiday so conservative estimate of 26k-13k=13k for investment x 15 years =195k plus interest. So probably 300k in 15years! Hopefully increased income & good investments will boost it to the $1,000,000 k figure in 15 years!	Third Highest Priority	6
10 Years	Become millionaire? Too vague and unlikely with so many other things going on so nice if it happens, but more focus on other aspects!		Lowest Priority	7
10 Years	Own a million dollar house! Sounds great but again unrealistic. Since our focus is on wealth generation I would be more inclined to invest in some kind of property. Since we are paying out $800 a month in rent, if somewhere along the way we can buy a property, with the same outlay that would be ok otherwise forget it for now!		No Priority	0
Anytime	Travel by land and boat from Spain to South Africa over a period of a year, and write a book about the adventure!			8

So here, in this exercise, the Ricardo's took a deeper look at their 'Silly Wish Reduction Exercise' and picked out the tricky items, in order to examine them. Obvious areas such the fast track MBA course, were not included, simply because it's obvious and does not provide any confusion. However, where there is doubt or uncertainly, simply put the items into the 'Priority Planner' and do the math!

The first section outlines the timeframe, which is followed by a description, which is filled in by the stakeholders, and then a description of priority. Once the list is completed, simply read through the list and place a number beside each goal, beginning with 1 for the most important goal and then moving on down the list adding numbers each time.

So in the example above, the kids' college fund comes up as number 3, because it is really important for the Ricardo's to have enough money, to send their kids to college in about 7 years' time. As for the least important goal it comes in as number 5, which is becoming a millionaire.

It's not that the Ricardo's won't become millionaires, it rather that they are focusing on other matters first. So the kids education and other practical matters come first for them, if possible they will also achieve the goal of becoming millionaires in the 10 year time frame, if not it's still ok, because at least the family is achieving the things which need to be achieved, and without going into debt!

So the idea behind this exercise is to weed out the pie in the sky stuff and create a list of goals, which are both believable and doable, which means goals which you can buy into and which you can also achieve. Remember it's easy to shoot for a goal which is exciting, but which is not really doable, however, you will only end up getting frustrated at your apparent inability to succeed.

By the same token, it can be easy to take on a goal which is doable, but which will not interest you, it's not something which you believe in, in which case when you have the goal it will feel bitter sweet, rather than feeling a sense of accomplishment, it will result in disillusionment, that you invested so much effort to achieve something which you did not really believe in, in the first place!

The idea behind this series of exercises, from the blue sky thinking, initial financial overview exercise, to the silly wish reduction exercise and finally the prioritization exercise, is simply to expand your mind into investigating all the possible areas of interest. This is really about seeking out goals which appeal to you, then reducing the goals down to what you believe in and finally selecting goals which are doable in the real World.

Just take a look at the diagram below, it outlines in a visual way, the points which have been raised in this section. We begin with a very big inverted triangle; this reveals the enormous range of possibilities, which is blue sky thinking.

This allows for the possibility of acknowledging interests, and potentially goals which you never realized as being there at all. While this is good, we need to reduce this down a bit, via the 'Silly Wish Reduction' exercise; this is where we get rid of all the pie in the sky stuff and reduce down to a series of goals which you believe are reachable and which you have a belief in, and that they interest you. Finally with the prioritization list we reduce still further, until we are only focusing upon the few goals, in hand, which we are going to focus our limited resources on achieving!

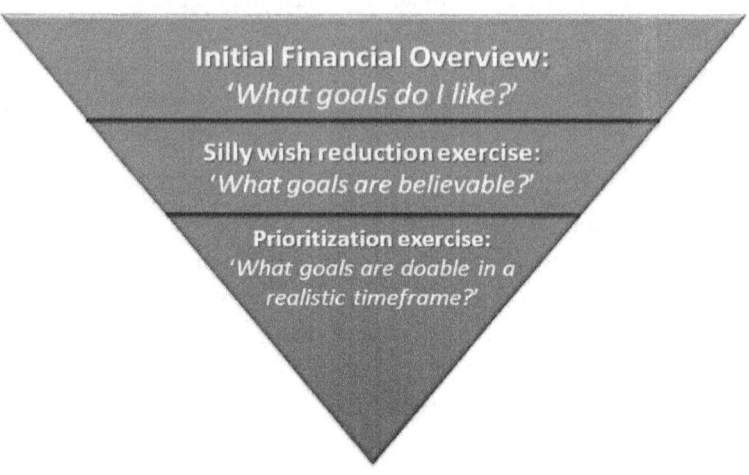

These are the doable goals, those which you believe that you can achieve in the real World and in a real-time scale. Finally the flow of these exercises, although apparently simple, has been designed in such a way, that you work through blue sky thinking, then onto believable goals and finally onto achievable ones.

Goal Finding and Prioritization Exercise Flow

The importance of Believable and Achievable Goals

134

If we arranged the exercise in a different manner, we could have begun with achievable goals, instead of believable ones, however, then you would be setting yourself up to pursue goals which you can do, but which you might have no interest in!

I cannot emphasize this point enough; reach for the stars, then narrow your focus down to that, which interests you, and finally do some reality checking and pursue that which is both believable and achievable, in a realistic timeframe. This is the key to achieving goals, which will both excite you and result in a positive biofeedback loop!

You may well like to reach for the stars, and a great many self-help books will suggest this. However, without a plan of action, which is both believable and achievable, then how do you hope to achieve anything at all!

I have met so many people, who bought into 'the power of positive thinking' and now the latest crazes, which are 'the law of attraction', and 'the power of intention', and yet they have achieved nothing, and now feel disillusioned!

It's not that any of these principals are in error, but rather it is a case of action. No matter how good ones life philosophy might be, without an action plan it will never take off from the ground. It's like owning the World's best sports car, and yet never taking it out for a drive, what use is it to you!

Let's put it another way, a millionaire entrepreneur might try and explain to a novice entrepreneur, the secret to their success, however, unless the novice entrepreneur goes out and performs action, nothing will happen, no matter how good the advice!

Furthermore, as any trainer will tell you, it's not enough to tell a student the correct steps to follow; rather the trainer or teacher has to outline a methodology, which is both believable and achievable, on the part of the student.

By way of a tangible example, a student goes to learn how to skydive, and invariably on the first dive, the instructor goes piggyback, whereby the instructor is tied to the student. Throughout the exercise, the instructor is in full control, all of the time. However, the skydive instructor could probably easily outline to the student how to do a free fall dive, first time out, but why then will they not do this?

The answer lies not with the instructor, but rather it lies with the student. The instructor cannot go beyond what the student believes they can achieve nor can they go beyond what is achievable, for the student, with their present level of experience. Hence all teaching begins at a slow pace, until the student gets the hang of things.

I am not suggesting that you give up on 'the law of attraction' or any other novel way of approaching life situations. However, I strongly suggest that every new skill requires time to learn, as well as to believe in the skills which you have acquired; and both to these things can only be achieved, via a slow and deliberate application of these new patterns. So that after a while, they become second nature and are easy for you to have belief in their efficacy.

Returning to goals, start off with something which is both believable and achievable considering your present circumstances. Then take out massive action to achieve this goal. Even a small goal, once achieved will result in greater belief in what you are doing and confidence in your abilities to actualize the goal.

Furthermore, remember that goals are always flexible, as one set of goals becomes easy, and then simply change the goals!

A novice car driver might at first feel intimidated, just taking their car out onto the main road, however after some time, they might laugh to themselves when they remember back at their early car driving efforts, and may well be amazed at just how easy they now find driving to be.

The novice car driver example is a good one, because most of us can drive, and anyone who can drive will easily remember just how difficult the first driving lessons where, and yet here we are now, driving everywhere, with absolute ease!

Sadly what's obvious, in a tangible away is not obvious in a subtle, way. We can all get the driver example; however, most of us have very limited experience, when it comes to actualizing our goals!

Just remember, to take the same approach when it comes to pursuing goals, that you took to learning to drive your car, or cycle your bike!

Begin with simple principles and then take action, and amend as necessary!

If you want to become a millionaire, why not try manifesting some simple things first and then go for the big stuff! Remember you can always start small and amend goals as need be, to tie in with your increased skills (achievability) and increased confidence in your ability to manifest (believe)!

Take massive Action!

Probably one of the most important lessons which I learned, during my time as a salesman, was the importance of massive action. Sales people are always judged, according to results delivered within a limited timeframe.

Most sales people are judged according to how much money they bring into an organization, usually in a timescale of one month, although this can vary, for example an airplane salesman may be judged on how many planes they can sell over a two or three year long period.

However, whichever way you look at it, sales people always have to achieve certain goals, within a certain timescale.

After a fair amount of time, working in sales, I began to realize how some sales people were making the grade and yet many others were not getting anywhere. And yet more often than not, most sales people have the same tools are their disposal; as in they are selling the same products as other sales people in the same organization, and usually the more successful sales people where no more charming or charismatic than the failing sales people.

So, what's the biggest difference between the top performers and the losers?

Well first of all, the top sales people were always very competitive; so let's put this to one aide for the moment, since every human being is not competitive. So what other winning traits did they have?

Well the clear winner by a mile was massive action!

If, say for example, a great sales person only makes 100 prospective calls in a month, even if they have a 10% closing ratio, it still only equates to 10 sales a month. However, a far inferior sales person, who only has a 5% closing ratio, if they make 500 calls in a month, will still manage to close 25 sales in a month! This is a result of taking massive action!

Another realization, which dawned on me after a while, was that companies would usually give a sales person two or three months to proof themselves, after which time they would sack the offending sales person. Initially this looks obvious, but if we analyze it, a little bit more deeply, we can see that a company has to get a return from the sales person.

Otherwise, not only are they not bringing in new sales, but they are also costing the company money, as in wasted resources which have been provided to the sales person, such as admin staff allocated to the sales persons, waste of managerial time overviewing the sales persons, a salary in many cases, a company car or laptop in other cases.

Because of these possible downsides, which result from retaining an ineffectual sales person, businesses can only afford to provide the opportunity for new sales people, of working in that organization, for a period of two or three months, without achieving their targets !

If the sales person fails to make the grade, in this timespan, then the company has no other choice than to revoke the opportunity away from the sales person.

This may sound obvious; however, there is a principal at work here, in that every opportunity in life has a limited shelf life. For sales people it is quite obvious, it's as if a very large hour glass were set up in their office. But instead of an hour to finish its sand, this hour glass takes a month, or longer, for the sand to transverse its way through the glass.

With each passing day, there is less time to reach their target, and if they miss their target, then the pressure starts coming on, and if it drags on long enough, without reaching their target, the sales person loses their job!

Ok, so let's expand a little beyond the sales person and think of life in general, and about our unique life problems, in particular. In a way the salesman's dilemma is everyone's dilemma. For example, most people need to make a certain amount of progress in their career.

For corporate executives, for example, who have not made it into management by age 40, they will probably have a very limited scope for career growth, in their respective organizations, because there is a presumption, from their superiors that an executive make the leap into management in their 20's or 30's at the latest!

Another example is the timeframe to get married. While people get married, at all sorts of ages, most people will find their ability to attract new partners diminishes with age, until a point is reached whereby it becomes difficult, although not impossible, to achieve marital status.

Then of course, there is the example of health. A person who has been diagnosed with some serious health condition, such as sclerosis of the liver, may well be able to turn things around, if they take correct action immediately. However, a point will come when the liver can no longer be repaired and at this stage only a replacement will, do!

Take a look around at your own life, and the people whom you know, and it becomes quite easy to see that each of us is faced with challenges, which while not being insurmountable, require appropriate action with a limited timeframe, after which stage, if we have not fulfilled this action, then we are forced to let go of this opportunity!

Of course one lost opportunity is not the end of everything, after all as long as there is breath in our bodies, we can always strive after new opportunities, however, each opportunity has only a limited shelf life, and if we are not careful, perhaps all the opportunities in a given area will dry up.

The classic examples are the Casanova who has fun with lots of girls, and even meets some really nice ladies and yet because he doesn't want to commit, they drift away. Years later he wants to settle down, with a nice girl, only to find that it never works out for him.

Another classic example is the sportsman or woman who has an injury only to find that after they have recovered from the injury that they are no more in demand, due to their increased age, even though they only are in their mid-thirties!

The examples are endless, but whichever way you look at it, there are only ever a limited number of opportunities in a given direction. While, it's true that possibilities are endless, it's the specific opportunities which have a shelf life!

So what happens when we apply this kind of thinking to somebody who wants to get out of debt, or who wants to attain great wealth?

What it means is that whatever circumstance, in which we find ourselves; this set of circumstances has a shelf life too. For example, say you owe $100,000 and have at your disposal $3,000 a month, which you can set aside to pay of the outstanding debt.

If you get stuck into it, it is possible to clear this debt, even if it is high interest debt, within a few years, if you want to. However, what if you don't take massive action?

If instead, you only pay off $2,000 a month, for example. In that case it could easily take you double the timespan, in order to clear off the debt. Then again what if you pay $3,000 this month and only $1,000 next month, will it ever be cleared? Well probably not!

So, by not taking massive action, your credit card debt will remain a constant in your life. Now it's not the end of the World, if you cannot clear it off, however, it does restrict you, because how can you possibly move onto wealth creation, without clearing your debts first!

Again back to the example of the failing salesman. Let's say he only turns in 10 sales a month, when he needs 15 sales to reach his target. Really he has got two options, which are to both increase his activity levels and make more prospecting calls, or he has to leave the job.

The World won't stand still because he doesn't take massive action, nor will he never receive any opportunities in future, it isn't like that. We each receive many opportunities a day, regardless of age, educational standard or quality of health. However, we are only finite creatures, with a lifespan which most find to be a little bit on the short side.

If you do not take massive action today, yes you will have new opportunities tomorrow however, they might not be as good as the opportunities which you have got today! And once they have slipped by, maybe no similar opportunity will come your way again!

For all the great self-help concepts, which are doing the rounds, it is this concept of 'taking massive action' which is the least applied, simply because most of us like to be couch potatoes. We have been raised in a culture, whereby it is more comfortable to sit still and be taken for granted, rather than to stick our heads up out of the trenches.

Yes of course, if you stick your head up, it might be knocked off, but then again if you stay down in the dirt you will have s**t up to your neck, and you will have no other choice than to just get on with it!

Taking massive action is never easy. As human beings we are filled with many fears and uncertainties, and to shake ourselves out of our stupor and go that extra mile, will always push us beyond our comfort zone. However, if you really want to change your life, then do think in terms of taking massive action.

Just like goal setting, you can go at your own pace, it is not necessary to go way beyond your limits. However, by pushing out the boundaries a little each day, over time this action builds and builds until great results will surely come your way!

Consequently, in practice it is better to set a small goal, and then pursue it enthusiastically, rather than to set a huge goal and never do anything about it.

After all we are creatures of habit, just remember it took bad habits to bring you into your present state, and it will take some good habits to bring you back out into a better state.

Finally, take heart if you find, during introspection, that many chances have been wasted and that your lack of taking massive action has cost you dearly. While we can never bring back yesterday, there is always tomorrow, and who knows what may happen in the future. Don't waste your energies brooding over what is lost, rather set your mind forward and start applying your will today, by taking massive action from now on!

Carry out an Action Plan with the Short/medium Term Goals

Ok so you now have a series of short to medium term goals, which are believable and doable, and you have a timeframe in which to action them, so what next?

As we all know only too well, it is easy to create goals yet it is difficult to action them. Just take the famous New Year's resolutions for instance, hundreds of millions of people create New Year's resolutions and yet what a tiny percentage actually achieved anything with them?

I remember only too well, that a gym which I used to frequent would suddenly swell to overflowing, from January the second every year, and that this would continue until around March or early April at the latest. Nearly all of these enthusiastic gym goers would begin the year intent upon revamping their physiques, and yet the vast majority of them would give up on the idea within three to four months.

For myself, and the other regulars of the gym, this post-Christmas, post New Year's resolutions influx of gym members, was simply a yearly encumbrance, which would sort itself out once the new gym members ran out of steam!

While this might have been irritating for me and the other regulars, at the gym, the last thing which you want, is to take such pains to create goals and only to give up on them within a short time period!

So what to do about it?

Well first of all, remember that these goals are not the wish washy stuff of New Year's resolutions! Rather you have taken the time, and the energy, out to examine your thoughts and feelings in depth; you have selected goals, which are believable and doable, and you have set a realistic timeframe.

All of these factors, represent a significantly improvement upon the atypical goals, which most people set themselves. So already you are half way towards fulfilling your goals, simply by selecting and defining the correct goals with the right parameters, in the first place!

So all that remains now is to action those goals!

The importance of Reverse Engineering

The best way, to action a goal, is to break it down into smaller pieces, each of which can be auctioned and assessed as you go on. As the saying goes, 'how do you eat an elephant?' the answer is 'by eating little pieces at a time!' So this little bit of wisdom also applies to the completion of goals!

So take a goal and see what it is that needs to be achieved and then simply do some reverse engineering, so that you can see what it is that needs to be achieved and then work back towards the beginning, in order to see what steps need to be carried out.

Take, for example, the Ricardo's intention to save $100,000 for their kids' education within seven years. For the Ricardo's to achieve this goal, they will have to make some regular savings, but how much exactly?

In a simple way to work out this target, they can simply divide $100,000 by 7 and it gives a yearly target of $14,285. Of course they will place the money in some kind of investment vehicle, and the interest accrued could be worked out via a compound interest calculator, in which case they will simply enter the figure for year one, and then add compound interest to it, before adding next year's figure and so on.

However, to keep things simple!

For now let's presume the figure of $14,285 is a constant, and that whatever interest that they accrue on top of this amount of money, will merely keep up with inflation.

The Ricardo's need to save $14,285 a year for seven years, which breaks down as a figure of $1,190 a month. The end goal is $100,000, which via reverse engineering breaks down into a saving of $1,190 a month, over a timeframe of 84 months. So all the Ricardo's have to do, is to make a point of setting aside $1,190 a month and maintain a record of this figure!

Life being what it is, there is no exact way to forecast what the value of $1,190 a month will be, when placed into various interest accruing accounts over a period of 7 years. After all, interest rates vary, inflation varies and so forth. Seven years from now the equivalent to $100,000, because of inflation may be $110,000 or perhaps it will be $130,000, it's difficult to say how high or how low inflation will be over that time frame.

Also it's hard to predict how well investments will go during that time period. However one thing is for sure, the final figure will be very close to the target which the Ricardo's have set as a target for their children's educational fund.

Maybe the inflation adjusted figure will be perhaps $115,000, and possibly the Ricardo's $1190, when invested over time, comes to a figure of only $110,000. So, maybe they don't quite hit target, but who cares!

One thing is for sure, if you can discipline yourself to put aside a significant amount of money, each and every month, and place it into medium to long-term investments, great things will occur. Whether you reach your goals, or over achieve your goals a little bit, or under achieve a little bit, doesn't really matter! At least you will have achieved far more than most people ever will!

The point to take on board here is that the future is never fixed; fulfilling exact goals is almost impossible, unless your goals are very unambitious. However, if you set forth an ambitious goal and more or less achieve it, then more power to you!

There is no exact way to predict the future, but one thing is certain, that if you can make a habit of saving, great things will happen. Most parents, for example, do not manage to accrue a significant educational fund for their children.

In fact most will end up going into debt, in order to put their kids through college. Just think how empowering it must be to know in advance that your kids will be alright, and that even if you retire or get sick, that their educational needs will be fulfilled!

This sort of power, which comes from the proper allocation of goals and the willingness to action them, over the medium to long-term!

The same applies to each goal, simply carry out some reverse engineering on it and, basically break down the big goal into a series of smaller goals. Saving $100,000, for example, sounds like a fantastic figure, whereas saving $1,190 a month sounds quite doable. So simply break down the bigger goal into achievable chunks.

Also, do make a reality check, prior to launching an action plan for a new goal. For instance, maybe you have decided that you would like to save $50,000 in five years, and have calculated that in order to save this amount of money, that it requires a deposit of $833 a month.

Now, this is all well and good, but please do a quick check, to make sure that this is an amount of money which you can definitely spare, each and every month, because, usually our home finances work out more costly than we think.

It is better to set a lower figure, which you know that you can save, each and every month, rather than going for a figure which is a little on the high side.

While it's great to have an ambitious goal, the most important thing is to get into the habit of setting and achieving goals. As one goal is achieved, you can always create a new higher level goal and so on. Forward momentum is the main thing to keep in mind. Get into the habit of moving forward with your life, and maintain this momentum, and great things will be achieved.

Also break the main goal down into smaller goals, then keep track of those smaller goals and give some kind of reward as you clear each mini-goal. So, for example, with the goal of saving $100,000, this could be reduced down to 10 mini-goals of $10,000 each.

As for a reward, perhaps to set aside a smaller percentage figure and provide a treat of some kind. Perhaps $200 for a day out with the family, or if you want some bigger kick-back, then go for a higher figure, such as $500 and maybe make a really big day out or weekend away, as a form of reward. The reward figure will vary from individual to individual, so it's really up to you what figure to set, because it has to be motivational. By the same token, don't go mad and start spending significant chunks of your savings, or you will have no savings left!

While the reward system may sound a little wild, it's all about positive feedback. Just cast your mind back to the earlier figures, number 4 and 5 respectively. Here we see that the difference between someone who is in debt and another person who is wealthy, or at least moving towards wealth in the allocation of their resources. It's not the amount of resources which matter but rather the allocation of resources which matter. The first steps towards wealth, involve the settling up of outstanding debts, and an orchestrated plan has to be created and acted upon to achieve this.

Once you have become debt free, the emphasis shifts towards settling aside some of the resources, which have now been set free as a result of the debt reduction process, and then redirecting them into the pursuit of dreams, for example, such as creating a $100,000 college fund for your kids!

The Necessity of Reward Spending

Now it takes an advanced level of emotional maturity to set aside resources (as in terms of money) and direct it towards goals, whether they are short, medium or long term in nature. The World in which we live, is full of temptations which are directed at separating us from our money, and regardless of the worthiness of our goals, unless we can motivate ourselves, it can become difficult to stay on track, especially when we are attempting to juggle multiple goals and get on with the struggles of everyday life at the same time.

This is where rewards come in to play; while on one level they appear to waste money, in actual fact they create positive feedback and that's really important!

Most of us fall into debt in the first place is because of three reasons:

- Financial Ignorance
- Denial
- Comfort Spending

Financial ignorance is commonplace, because we have absolutely no organized educational programs on financial awareness. There might be the odd ad-hoc program, here or there, however, there is little or no education at high school level, which is the right time and place to be teaching these concepts. Also some schools might pay some lip service to financial awareness, in their social educational programs, however financial awareness should be the number one priority, for tenth to twelfth grade students, ahead of all other academic programs.

Why so?

Because, as soon as kids graduate from high school, they enter the adult World and very quickly they will fall into either good or bad financial habits. For many individuals, their financial problems actually begin at this age. Just imagine how many of us could have been spared, so much financial strife, if we only received some good quality practical financial education, during high school!

As a consequence, of this lack of financial now how, most adults are actually in denial of their financial situation. Personal finance is a big mystery to most people, and whenever they think about it, they tend to feel a little bit mystified and possibly even distraught.

This situation is not helped, when the said individual goes to seek financial advice from their local bank or brokerage service, which all too quickly gets them to invest their hard earned cash, in an equally mysterious financial vehicle, which may or possibly may not make them any money!

Over time, as a result of this state of denial, the debts begin to crop up, because without a good financial plan, spending will always go out of control. And this situation is further worsened by the tendency to comfort spend, in an effort to cheer ourselves up. It's all too easy to buy nice shiny new things on a credit card, or to go on a nice vacation, however come Monday morning and the bills are awaiting us!

This becomes a negative feedback loop, whereby our financial situation drifts out of control, we don't know what to do about it and then of course we tend to down play the situation, and hope it all goes away. Denial sets in, comfort spending comes back into play and the debt cycle goes around and around, all over again.

Now, we wish to use this same aspect of human psychology, in a positive way via positive feedback, whereby we set achievable targets, however small they may be, and we achieve them. Bit by bit our debts go down, and finally they disappear. Then little bit by little bit, our wealth increases, and first small goals are achieved, and then larger goals begin to be met also.

To help us stay on track, with motivation, we introduce the concept of a rewards system, whereby we give ourselves a little pat on the back. So, instead of comfort spending, we now have rewards spending, which is a much better situation to be in!

Ok, with these two considerations (reverse engineering for goal success, and the necessity of reward spending), out of the way let's take a closer look at the final stages of goal prioritization.

Let's take a look at the Ricardo's goals and how they are monitoring progress with them.

Summary of Goals for the Ricardo Family

Goal	Priority	Timeframe	Short/medium/Long Term
To be free of all debts within two years	1	2 years	Short-term
Family holiday to Europe will require around $6,000. Also thereafter we want to set aside $3,000 for a family holiday each year!	2	2 years	Short-term
Take up fast track MBA program, once debts are cleared	3	3 years	Medium-term
Consider career change, once debts cleared, would like to set up some sort of travel business?	4	2 years	Short-term
$100,000 college fund for the kids. Requires 10k a year investment	5	7 years	Medium-term
$1,000,000 investment (not likely) for now, first 7 years only we will be spending $10,000 on kids college fund (plus it will need to be topped up in college) and $3,000 for holiday. Conservative estimate of 26k-13k=13k for investment x 15 years =195k plus interest. So probably 300k in 15years! Hopefully increased income and good investments will boost it to the $1,000,000 figure in 15 years!	6	15 years	Long-term
Become millionaire? Too vague and unlikely with so many other things going on! Nice if it happens, but more focus on other aspects!	7	10 years	Long-term
Travel by land and boat from Spain to South Africa over a period of a year, and write a book about the adventure!	8	Anytime	Long-term
Hillwalking	9	Anytime	Anytime
Own a million dollar house! Sounds great but again unrealistic. Since our focus is on wealth generation, we would be more inclined to invest in some kind of property. Since we are paying out $800 a month in rent, if somewhere along the way we can acquire a property, with the same outlay then that would be ok, otherwise forget it for now!	10	Anytime	Anytime

Ok, when cited in this fashion, their goals appear to be both lengthy and eclectic. So first off, let's take a quick overview of the goals and the priorities. As we can see the priorities and timeframes vary widely, but in quick summary, getting rid of debt quickly and progressing their careers, are the highest priority, with one exception and that's the family holiday, which is an important reward after all the years of struggling to get rid of debt.

Following on from this come the goals of accumulating money, for the kid's college fund, then the focus moves onto wealth creation, and finally the wish list stuff, such as travelling the World and so on, comes into play.

So, How Do You Monitor so Many Diverse Goals?

Well let's take a look below…

First of all, some of these goals have a fairly low priority and are really more desires than goals. These include hillwalking, travelling around the World, becoming a millionaire and owning a million dollar house.

It's not that they are unimportant; rather it's just that they are less important than the more tangible goals, which have taken centre stage for the Ricardo's.

Simply put, there are only so many resources (whether they are financial or time resources), so it's simply not possible to focus on everything at once. Also over a period of time many goals will change, consequently the real emphasis here is simply to make progress on the central goals, which will move one's life forward.

Other goals can be added, adapted or deducted as time moves on!

So focusing then on the remaining six goals, let's takes a look at the Ricardo's first goal monitoring Worksheet...

Goal Monitoring Worksheet for the Ricardo's 2015-2016

Month	Date	Credit Card Payment	Overdraft Facility	Auto loan
1	Nov-12	$1552	$300	$325
2	Dec-12	$1552	$300	$325
3	Jan-13	$1552	$300	$325
4	Feb-13	$1552	$300	$325
5	Mar-13	$1552	$300	$325
6	Apr-13	$1552	$300	$325
7	May-13	$1552	$300	$325
8	Jun-13	$1552	$300	$325
9	Jul-13	$1552	$300	$325
10	Aug-13	$1552	$300	$325
11	Sep-13	$1552	$300	$325
12	Oct-13	$1552	$300	$325
13	Nov-13	$1552	$300	$325
14	Dec-13	$1552	$155	$325
15	Jan-14	$1552	0	$625
16	Feb-14	$1552		$625
17	Mar-14	$1552		$625
18	Apr-14	$1552		$625
19	May-14	$1552		$625
20	Jun-14	$1552		$625
21	Jul-14	$1552		
22	Aug-14	0		

Let's take a look at the Ricardo's debt profile once again:

Debt Type	Debt Amount	Min Payments
Credit Card One	$14,600	$292
Credit Card Two	$8,600	$172
Credit Card Three	$4,400	$88
Auto loan	$7,800	$325
Overdraft Facility	$3,800	$300
Total Debt	$39,200	
Total minimum Payments	$1,177	

The Ricardo's initial 'Goal Monitoring Worksheet' focuses upon just one goal, which is debt clearance. This is number 1 on their list, because they have more than $39,000 in debt and minimum payments off $1,177 a month is a big drag for them.

So initially this has to be cleared, also because the credit cards have high interest they have to be cleared first, so here is the strategy which the Ricardo's are following:

Their credit card debt is $27,600, with an average interest rate of 15%, and a minimum payment of $552 per month. By setting aside a $1,000 extra this debt can be cleared within 21 months.

The overdraft will clear within 14 months at the rate of $300 a month, and by adding the $300 which is freed up to the car repayment resulting in the auto loan being cleared within 20 months. So a total repayment time of 21 months!

Now let's take a look at the Ricardo's second Goal monitoring Worksheet…

Goal Monitoring Worksheet for the Ricardo's

September 2014-Decmeber 2015

Month	Holiday in Europe	Fastback MBA program	Consider career change	$100,000 College fund	$1,000,000 investment fund
	Save $2,000 per month for first 3 months. Save $500 per month for next years holiday when MBA paid for	Fees $6,000. Save $500 per month starting from 4th month. Then divert this amount to next years holiday fund	This goal will have to wait till others are acheived or income increases	Save $1,190 per month from 4th month	Total fund available is $2,127 per month. Will save $437 per month from 4th month
Sep-14	$2,000				
Oct-14	$2,000				
Nov-14	$2,000				
Dec-14	$6,000 saved for holiday in Europe	$500		$1,190	$437
Jan-15		$500		$1,190	$437
Feb-15		$500		$1,190	$437
Mar-15		$500		$1,190	$437
Apr-15		$500		$1,190	$437
May-15		$500		$1,190	$437
Jun-15		$500		$1,190	$437
Jul-15		$500		$1,190	$437
Aug-15		$500		$1,190	$437
Sep-15		$500		$1,190	$437
Oct-15		$500		$1,190	$437
Nov-15		$500		$1,190	$437
Dec-15	$500			$1,190	$437
Totals	$500 saved towards next years holiday	$6,000 paid for MBA Course		$15,470 saved for kids college fund	$5,681 saved for investment fund

So in the second 'Goal monitoring Worksheet', we see the Ricardo's pay for their European holiday, pay off a one year fastback MBA program, save $15,470 towards their kids' education and save a modest $5,681 towards long range savings. Finally they also reallocated the $500 which they were spending on the MBA program towards next year's holiday.

Now it must be remembered that the Ricardo's have undergone absolutely no change in circumstances. All that has happened is that they now have $2,127 free per month, which used to go towards paying off their debts. Secondly, they have made a concerted effort to redirect that money into constructive areas.

Let's take a look a one more 'Goal monitoring Worksheet', which will cover yet another year of their lives:

Goal Monitoring Worksheet for the Ricardo's

January 2016-December 2016

Date	Holiday	Consider career change	$100,000 College fund	$1,000,000 Investment fund
	Save $500 per month until $3,000 is attained. Start again in November for next year.	John receives promotion and extra $1,000 per month. Verona starts new business, while keeping up her present job. She needs $2,000 to launch in March which comes from 2 months of John's increase. Business will cost $500 per month to run initially.	Continue saving $1,190 per month	$500 of John's extra income can go to supplementing the travel business and the other $500 can go into long-term savings after the business is set up. When the holiday is paid for ($3,000) an additional $500 per month is placed in the investment fund until November when they start saving for the next year's holiday.
Jan-16	$500		$1,190	$437
Feb-16	$500	$1,000	$1,190	$437
Mar-16	$500	$1,000	$1,190	$437
Apr-16	$500	$500	$1,190	$937
May-16	$500	$500	$1,190	$937
Jun-16	$2,500 + $500	$500	$1,190	$1,437
Jul-16	From Last Year	$500	$1,190	$1,437
Aug-16		$500	$1,190	$1,437
Sep-16		$220	$1,190	$1,437
Oct-16		$100	$1,190	$1,437
Nov-16	$500	$300	$1,190	$937
Dec-16	$500	$400	$1,190	$937
Totals	$1,000	$4,720-$800 = $3,920	$14,280	$12,244
Previous year savings			$15,470	$5,681
			$29,750	$17,925

To summarize, the Ricardo's third 'Goal monitoring Worksheet', John Ricardo managed to get a promotion, in work which resulted in an increase in take home income of $1,000 per month. Also by April they had finished paying for their holiday, and beginning, in November, they began to save for the following year's holiday.

With the increased income, Verona Ricardo has decided to launch a corporate travel business, in a low key manner, by taking flexi-time in her job and using that time to email, phone and visit various travel companies and corporate offices, in an effort to create a corporate travel business.

Because she is starting in a low key way, her income is not affected, rather they just have to save $2,000 to launch the business and allocate $500 a month to operate it. As we can see by the figures, she is starting to make a small amount of income starting off in September, and more than likely by early 2016 she will be turning a profit on her business and will no longer require the $500 a month supplementation.

The children's college fund simply rolls on just like last year, because it is a major priority, since their kids need that money within the next few years.

Finally, the long-term investment fund is much more flexible since it has a 15 year timespan, and the Ricardo's are hoping to increase the amount of money, which they set aside to this fund on a yearly basis. As we can see the amount this fund receives varied from $437 to $1437 a month, depending upon circumstances.

Taking a quick overview, of the Ricardo's first three Goal monitoring Worksheets, we see them clearing off $39,200 in debts, we see John Ricardo paying for and completing an MBA program and managing to land a $12,000 a year, after tax, pay rise, We also see Verona Ricardo launch a part–time travel business; we see the family take a holiday to Europe and a regular holiday every year; we see them save $29,750 towards their kids' college expenses, and $17,925 towards their long term investments!

This is a lot of progress, and while none of it sounds very exciting they manage to achieve all of these things within a four year time frame!

It just goes to show, how regular coordinated steps can result in terrific progress over time. The thing to remember is that making progress towards life goals takes time. Something as low key as $500 a month can sound like a small amount, but over a period of months and years it can accumulate to quite a significant sum of money!

Also, the volume of cash flow is not so important either. In the example of the Ricardo's, they are on good salaries, and their debts are not so high, whereas many people will have lower incomes and higher debts. If you have been reading this book, possibly you might conclude that on your 'measly salary', no such progress could ever be made!

However, while the example of the Ricardo's was set in such a way, so as to illustrate how people, who are even on good salaries can have financial troubles, it must also be realized that progress can be made, in all cases. If your debts are really bad, perhaps you can consider debt consolidation or settlement. If they are not so bad, you can still clear your debts and accumulate wealth, even on a 'measly salary', however, you will have to be really patient.

So maybe rather than have a big turn-around in your finances, it might take seven or eight years instead of three or four years to achieve this financial feat! However, like I noted earlier, even if it takes time to achieve such a feat, it is still a great achievement to clear of debt and accumulate wealth, regardless how long it takes to do this!

Of course, as a counter argument we can also accept the fact that the Ricardo's do not exist, rather they are ideal people, an example made up in an effort to outline some principals. In reality life will rarely move along so smoothly, even with a $2,000 financial buffer zone account.

While this is all well and good, it must be born in mind that these figures are purely for illustrative proposes only. No one can guarantee that there will not be upsets such as perhaps employment problems or health problems, perhaps to contend with. However, while a little idealized, the intention behind constructing the Ricardo's and making out these various worksheets, is not for you to copy them in parrot like fashion, but rather to inspire similar activity from yourself.

Looking back again at these worksheets, while they may be a little bit idealized, they are not dramatic in fashion, everything which has been achieved, has been achieved in a very sensible way. You can also achieve a similar result in your life!

If you have some setbacks, it might slow down the progress, but progress will be made nonetheless, and that's what it's all about!

As we can see from the example of the Ricardo's, by doing some in-depth research, by prioritizing and then setting out with an action plan, you can not only free yourself of debt, but also you can then move on and re-appropriate the money which has been saved into clearing debts and using this money for the pursuit of tangible goals instead!

Also some people will like more detail in their worksheets than has been outlined here, while many others will shriek as the prospect of creating the sort of detail wish has been outlined here! Well that's fine too, it's about the spirit of these activities, rather than a strict adherence to them that matters, adapt as needs be!

One thing which has always irked me is the tendency of some self-help programs, to focus too much on creating and following a very rigid plan. Creating perhaps, a 5 year plan and then breaking it down into 60 months and 260 weeks, and starting out the program with an intention perhaps to accumulate $100,000 in that timeframe and estimating that by week 140 they will have saved exactly $53,847!

Now let's get real here! It is really unlikely that you can save money or progress towards the fulfilment of your goals, in such a liner fashion, and it is just this kind of rigid thinking which can easily knock you off of your stride!

In reality life is very dynamic and often it can be quite challenging, so rather than having everything set in stone, we need to have a dynamic system in place, which helps us to move forward in a persistent manner. Progress even if it be slow, over time, as long as it is consistent will achieve results!

On the subject of challenges, Sylvester Stallone, in the guise of 'Rocky Balboa' makes a great speech in an effort to motivate his son in the movie 'Rocky Balboa', the last of the Rocky series of movies. The speech is all about facing up to challenges, and in particular he notes that:

> *"Nobody is going to hit as hard as life. But it isn't about how hard you hit, it's about how hard you can get hit and keep moving forward. How much can you take and keep moving forward? That's how winning is done."*

Well Sylvester Stallone hit it on the head! Life is all about dealing with setbacks, and yet somehow managing to keep moving forward. Although a few people achieve greatness, via luck or exceptional ability in a given arena, for the vast majority of human beings greatness is achieved by setting their minds on a particular goal and pursuing it with unnerving will!

There are a lot of self-help programs out there, which you can choose to follow, however where real success lies in not simply in following the program, but rather it lies in persistence, whereby we stay with the program. Furthermore, it is more important to stick with the principals, of the program, rather than following the program in a rigid manner.

With the five keys program, the intention from my side is to provide the reader, not only with a tangible system which they can deploy, but also in principals which are flexible enough to be adapted according to individual circumstances and timeframes. This is why, with the five pillar system, there is no focus on rigid timeframes, and on following a cookie cutter styled program.

Rather the intention, behind the five keys program, is for you to learn how to overview your life, to take stock of what needs to be changed and how to initiate change and then to provide guidance which can be easily adapted according to needs.

Taking a look at our mythical family again, the Ricardo's, we can see that they achieved a great deal, in four years, via the deployment of goal monitoring programs. If we look back at their original goals, we can see that over the next decade or so they will end up rolling out a goal monitoring program on average once a year, perhaps sometimes a little bit longer. Over this time frame, as one goal is achieved, it will drop of the worksheet and over time new goals will be added to the worksheet.

Ultimately, the goal monitoring program is simply for guidance purposes, and this is where many self-help programs get it wrong, because they emphasize the goal monitoring program, as if it were an end in and of itself, and this is simply not true, because the only reason for creating and following such a program, is in an effort to keep the achievement of goals on track.

Most human beings will simply fail to achieve anything of significance, unless they have some kind of goals to follow and some way of monitoring them. So, the aim is to achieve the goals, the goal monitoring program is only vehicle to get you there!

Remember, that the program is a vehicle and like any other vehicle it is only as good as it is useful! Deploy the five pillar program, in order to deliver results and adapt and change both the goals and the program, itself in order to achieve the goals. The goals are you dreams and the program is only a tool to assist you, in pursuing those dreams. Consequently, you must feel free, to adapt as need be as long as you are able to make progress

Finally, progress in financial terms is basically a marathon rather than a sprint. While there are some individuals, who manage to amass significant wealth in a very short period of time, by far the vast majority of wealthy individuals amass wealth over the medium to long-term. While wealth may not be your most important life goal, it will always play a significant part in our lives because of the necessity of money, in the World in which we live.

Furthermore, as we grow older we tend to need access to greater amounts of money because apart from anything else, when we get old, we need money to live on after we have finished our working lives, and as we become aged, medical expenses usually mount up. Also for those of us who have kids, they tend to cost ever greater amounts of money, until they finish college!

While it is great to follow the program, as laid down, if you really want to make the most of the money which you and your family are saving, then it is important to have some kind of long-term financial plan, so as to make the best returns on your investment, and this leads on nicely to the fifth pillar of credit card debt freedom!

Chapter Six - The Fifth Key to Debt Freedom – Creating Wealth

A plan to redirect the money which you have at your disposal, after paying off debt, where it can be redirected using financial planning to create the life which you really want for yourself and your family!

With the fifth pillar, we are focusing upon deploying good financial planning, after you have finished paying off credit card debt, in an effort to create a new level of financial wellbeing for yourself and your family.

By this stage, in the 5 pillars to credit card debt freedom program, we have covered a lot of ground. We have learned about the importance of refraining from adding new credit card debt, we have learned about the importance of budgeting, we have learned about keeping some money aside, in a financial buffer fund, so as to keep the debt reduction process on track, and we have learned about the importance of setting short to medium-range financial goals so that we will have something to aim for, which will help to keep the debt reduction process on track.

However, even when you have finished paying off debt, there is a new possibility open to you and your family, which is financial abundance. With good financial planning, it is possible to produce financial abundance in your life within the medium to long-term.

By shifting your focus, from paying off debt, to long term financial wellbeing, with the help of good financial planning, not only can you become debt free, and stay that way, but also a new life awaits you and your family, a life which is filled with financial abundance, which is the ultimate insurance protecting you against a relapse into credit card debt!

Going from Indebtedness to Financial Wellbeing

It may sound like an unrealistic aspiration, to seek to go from debt to financial abundance, but really there is very little that divides the wealthy from those who are in debt!

The major differences between the wealthy and the indebted are the focus of their financial beliefs and habits. Listed below are the different financial beliefs and habits which divide these two polar opposites:

Beliefs and Habits of the Indebted versus the Wealthy

The Indebted	The Wealthy
Financial Beliefs/ Habits	Financial Beliefs/habits
Short-term results/ Buy today - payback tomorrow	Long-term results/ Invest for the long-term
Follow the crowd/Get into debt	Stand apart from the crowd/ Become wealthy
No financial planning/ Finances going from bad to worse!	Good financial planning/ Finances constantly improving

While on the face of it, the indebted may appear radically different from the wealthy, when we take a closer look at it we can see that it's simply a matter of focus, which makes the difference between the two. In a nutshell, the indebted don't like to think about a timeframe, they do not like to get into financial planning, and they want immediate satisfaction today and demonstrate an unwillingness to wait for satisfaction. And this is the complete antithesis of the wealthy, who like financial planning and who are willing to put off immediate satisfaction, as long as the long-term results are worthwhile.

The vital thing, to understand here, is that that the wealthy are not necessarily those who have a big income. Indeed many credit card debtors are themselves quite well paid and should be wealthy, if they were sensible. However, it really does not matter how much income you have, if you manage to spend more than you earn, which is a very easy achievement in today's consumer driven society!

In reality, a significant proportion of the wealthy in society do not have a particularly large income, rather anyone can become wealthy if they get into financial planning. The only major difference between a wealthy person who has a big income, versus a wealthy person who has a small income is the timeframe which it will take them to accumulate wealth. For example, a person who has an income of $1,000, 000 per year, and who lives on a yearly budget of $500,000 will increase their savings by an enormous $500,000 per year.

Whereas someone who has a small income, and who can only save $500 a month, will only be able to put away $6,000 per year. So obviously, regardless how good they are at financial planning, it will take them a long time to accumulate wealth, but wealth will come in the long-term. The major difference will be that the first person, with an enormous income, could become wealthy in less than one year, whereas the person with a small income could take 20 years to become wealthy. But here is the important thing, by getting into financial planning, the investor with a small income will also manage to become wealthy, even if it takes them a long time to get there!

So the important point to realize here is that there is very little difference between the wealthy and the poor, rather the greatest difference lies in the focus. The wealthy think long-term and are willing to get into detailed financial planning, in order to create a wealth producing template, whereas the poor want instant gratification and are willing to get into debt as long as they get the gratification which they seek!

So, if you are in debt at the moment, obviously your first port of call is to free up your cash flow by paying off debt. Once you have finished paying off debt, you have an opportunity to become wealthy, if you are willing to do some financial planning and initiate some action!

Financial Planning in Practice

Hopefully by now I have convinced you of the reality that, with a little bit of financial planning, it is possible for you and your family to go from debt to wealth, even if it will take a little time. All it takes is a concerted effort, whereby by paying off debt, you then follow through with good financial planning and a willingness to initiate the action plan!

Of course, none of this will achieve anything for you unless the financial planning is appropriate for your circumstances. Sadly while your intentions may be good, unless you know what you are doing, chances are that the long-term results will be less than positive. Since there are so many financial products on the market today and a good many financial sales people, who are more than willing to sign you up to any program, which makes them good commission, financial planning can easily turn into an expensive and unrewarding experience.

The only way to guarantee success, with your financial planning, is to gain a good understanding of your unique financial situation, which includes such factors as monthly income, monthly expenses, long-term career goals, family circumstances, long-term financial prospects of the locality in which you live, and so on. So, it is not possible to come up with a generic answer, a one way fits-all template. Rather once you have finished paying off debt, it is necessary to take a detailed look at your life and aspirations and do some financial planning which will work specifically for you!

Fortunately, if you have been following the lessons outlined in the 5 pillars to credit card debt freedom, then you will already be well on the way to understanding most of the dynamics which are necessary for financial planning to be successful!

The central concept, that you need to understand, is that any brokers who you may talk too, and this includes your local friendly bank branch, are all out to make a commission form you and really they do not care much about how you do in the long-term. The only way for financial planning, to work well in the long-term, is for you to gain a detailed understanding of your unique circumstances and then to do the research to come up with a financial plan which will work for you.

Finally, you have to take stock, of your changing circumstances on a semi-annual basis, and make the necessary changes to your financial planning in order to amend the plan as needs be, so that your financial planning stays on track with your long-term financial goals!

First step in financial planning

Setting realistic financial goals

Going from paying off debt to becoming wealthy is not a walk in the park; if you want to make this implausible goal achievable, then it is necessary to begin with realistic goals. One of the greatest inhibitions to success is setting goals which are unrealistic, and this is where many self-help programs fail, because while they excite their participants, as long as their participants believe the financial goals to be unrealistic, they will unconsciously hold themselves back from success. So, by setting realistic goals, goals which are doable, it becomes fairly easy to fulfil them, and then fulfilment of small goals leads on quite naturally to the achievement of bigger and better goals!

So, how to set realistic financial goals?

Simply, begin by looking at the amount of disposable monthly income, which you have left after paying off debt, and decide on how much of this needs to be allotted to long-term financial goals, and how much do you want to keep aside for leisure goals. For the sake of simplicity in the fourth pillar, I mentioned a 50:50 split between leisure spending and long-term financial planning. Ultimately, it is up to yourself as to how much money to a lot to each activity; but my advice to you is to make sure that some money is put aside for your long-term financial wellbeing.

The good thing about paying off debt is that it helps you to rationalize your monthly expenditure and get into good budgeting habits. While paying off debt is not fun, if you have followed the lessons which have been presented in the 5 pillars, you will have learned a lot about budgeting and understanding the intricacies of you monthly expenses. Also, you will have streamlined the monthly expenses, thus saving yourself some money each month.

This actually puts you ahead of most people, who do not have a debt problem, because they are more than likely wasting money, because without the pressure of debts over one's head, the tendency is to waste money. This rationalized monthly budgeting, combined with the money which you now have at your disposal, once you have finished paying off debt, means that you now have a considerable potential investment fund at hand.

So looking, at the example, of a credit card debtor who has been paying off debt, to the sum of $1,000 a month, and who has learned to further reduce their outgoings by another $500 a month, they will probably be around $1,500 a month better off than most people with the same income, but who do not have a debt problem. The person, who is debt free, will probably be spending this $1,500 a month, without making any good financial planning and more than likely they will either waste this money or if they invest some of it, they will more than likely invest it wastefully!

So when we think about it, the best advantage of getting into financial planning, just after you have played off debt, is that you have become accustomed to living on far less than you earn each month. So before you accustom yourself to this extra income and start wasting it on discretionary expenditure, just take a stand and decide on setting aside a certain amount each and every month and putting it to good use via a financial planning program!

Once you have decided, upon how much you can realistically put aside, into an investment fund, each month then take an account of what it is that you want to achieve in the long-term and then come back to reality by comparing this to how much you can invest each month, at this stage. The important thing to understand is that while your long-term aim might be to become a millionaire, if you only have $500 a month to invest then it is unlikely that you can become a millionaire anytime soon. However, just because you can only set aside $500 a month today, does not mean that you will be limited to this figure forever!

So even though it may sound unreasonable to aim for great wealth, if you're disposable income is on the low side, just aim for some reasonable amount of medium to long-term wealth. Believe it or not simply by getting into the habit of financial planning and actioning an investment plan, however humble it may be, will help you to quickly improve your overall income levels!

So at this stage, do not get hung up on making 'gazillions', just set realistic goals and work towards them and be willing to upwardly revise them once they begin start to get actualized!

So how do I set my first financial goals?

Simply begin by looking at how much you can save each month, then multiply this figure by 12 months to come up with a yearly figure, then add in a realistic wage increment figure, and put that into next year's figure and then project this over a 10 year period. For example, the debtor with $500 a month disposal income will have $6,000 a year to invest. Next year if they add in a 5% increment, then they will have $6,300 a year to invest next year, and so on.

Simply roll out these figures into an excel sheet (If you don't have access to a computer, or just don't like working out figures on a computer, then buy a hardback mathematical notebook, and simply work out all these figures, with the help of a calculator, and then write them in by hand.) and you can quickly work out how much you can invest each year at these conservative figures; this way you know roughly speaking how much you can invest.

In an effort to make some projections, on these investment figures simply add in some rough compound interest return figures, and roll these over with the new investment figures. For example, the investor who has decided in their financial planning to invest $6,000 in year one, that if they presume a conservative compound interest figure, of 4% a year over 10 years, this will become $8881.47 over a ten year period. The year two figure, of $6,300 at 4% interest per year, will grow to become $ 8,966.86 within ten years. Now the easiest way to come up with these approximate figures, is to go online and search under 'compound interest calculator' and run the figures through them, and then add these figures to the excel sheet. Do this ten times, and you have an approximate 10 year return on investment projection!

Now these figures are approximates, because in reality if you are investing on a monthly basis, your interest levels will vary, also your conservative interest rate level may vary from year to year ,as will the rate of inflation, and so too will the percentage incremental increase in your monthly income over the years.

So you may well be thinking that since there are so many variables at hand,

why bother with projections at all?

While it is impossible to carry out really accurate financial planning, unless you make some projections you will have a hard time figuring our whether or not a particular long term financial planning strategy is right for you or not. Secondly, by carrying out, some financial planning projection figures, it can give you a rough idea as to how well you will be doing in the long-term. Finally, by creating approximate financial planning projections, you can inspire yourself to keep moving forward.

If you simply redirect your disposal income into long-term investments, it can be difficult to maintain motivation whereas, if you have a rough idea as to how you should be doing, it can help to maintain your motivation. Furthermore, it can be exciting and interesting to compare the projections against the reality of your financial planning efforts.

For inspirational purposes, take a quick look at the table below, which outlines the example quoted above:

Ten years Investment Example

Year	# Years Money is Invested for	Yearly Investment Sum	Total Amount at the End of the 10 Year Investment Cycle
1	10	6,000	8,881
2	9	6,300	8,966
3	8	6,617	9,055
4	7	6,948	9,143
5	6	7,295	9,230
6	5	7,660	9,319
7	4	8,043	9,409
8	3	8,445	9,499
9	2	8,867	9,591
10	1	9,310	9,682
Total	10	75,485	92,775

Remember this is not intended to be accurate, it's simply designed to give you a rough idea as to what you can expect to achieve, by following 10 years of investment at $6,000 of investment per year at an interest rate of 4% per year, and with an incremental increase in investments of 5% per year.

As you can see, even with this very conservative financial planning, the investor sees an accumulation of in excess of $92,000 in 10 years! Even if we take into consideration that this, very conservative interest level, is probably no higher than inflation, if we simply look at the investment amount rather than the investment amount plus interest, we still come up with a figure of $75,485.

So, even if we presume that this interest rate is no better than inflation, it still adds up to $75,485 in 10 years (presuming those 10 years from now that the figure of $92,775 is equivalent to $75485, when we take the inflation into account). So even with a conservative investment scheme, at the very least the investor manages to save their money and also to keep inflation at bay. Needless to say, without any radical changes, imagine how much this will add up to be in 20 years!

Consequently, if you are presently paying off debt, and wondering if financial planning will achieve anything useful for you in the long-term, now you know you that even with conservative financial planning, you can have 55k in your bank account in ten years' time!

And believe me if you follow, even a conservative financial planning scheme, like this one above, not only will you end up with a 5 digit figure in your bank account, but chances are that mysteriously your income will increase exponentially, because money begets money!

Also, I know that most self-help guides will suggest far more ambitious goals to strive for, over a 10 year period. I am not, for one minute, suggesting that you don't strive to achieve great things, but what I would suggest, is that when starting out begin with small goals and then revise upwards. Success in achieving a small goal is far more beneficial, for your self confidence levels, than failing at a big goal!

If you set out a conservative investment goal, such as the one above, and feel after a year or two, that it's very unambitious and that you are confident that a greater amount can be achieved, then simply revise upwards accordingly!

Finally, the main reason for featuring a conservative goal, like the one above, is simply to show you that even the most normal people, under average circumstances can achieve a great deal, simply by being persistent. I certainly hope that you can quickly improve your present circumstances, as in increase your income and career opportunities, but, even if for some reason this is not possible, right now, by being prudent, it is possible to clear off debt and save for the long-term!

Summary

So just too quickly summarize this section, on realistic goal setting. Don't get hooked into the mistake which most self-help programs propagate for their participants, of reaching for the stars. Simply follow a simple logical conservative investment plan, and stick to it regardless what happens, and little success will create bigger success. While you might have difficulty to imagine having $1,000,000 in the bank, if you don't believe in the possibility, it just will not happen, or even if it does happen it will not last long because unless you believe and accept in the possibility of having a certain level of wealth manifest in your life, your unconscious mind will simply sabotage your success!

This is exactly what we see in the case of so many people who win the lottery or who come into large sums of money, in an unexpected way, only to lose their financial windfall almost as quickly as they received it!

The best way to work your way towards a financial goal, which is seemingly impossible, is to begin which a much smaller goal and to build incrementally upon that. So if you have $10,000 in the bank, it becomes possible to imagine possessing $50,000. Then when you have $50,000, saving $100,000 starts to become realistic. When you have $100,000 in the bank, then the possibility of having $250,000 starts to appear achievable. So rather than focusing upon a huge figure, which is unbelievable to you, at this point in time, rather refocus and move onto the next goal.

Begin with financial goals which are a challenge, but which at the same time are doable in your eyes. Then keep on progressing until a stage is reached whereby it becomes possible to manifest the really big financial goals in your life!

So, if initially you decide that $1,000,000 in the bank is what you require, then cut this figure down to size and focus on achievable goals. So maybe your first goal might be $10,000, second goal might be $50,000, third goal might be $200,000, fourth goal might be $250,000, fifth goal might be $500,000, and then the sixth goal might be $1,000,000.

In the example of the Ricardo's who want to have $1,000,000 saved within fifteen years; they don't in reality have a plan in place to achieve this goal. Rather, initially they feel that $300,000 is a realistic figure based upon putting aside a fairly small amount of money each month, which is all that they feel that they can do, because they have to priorities towards saving money for their kids' college education, which is only seven years away.

However, while this may well be true, it must also be remembered that the Ricardo's are young, they are only in their early thirties, and are likely to increase their incomes in an exponential manner over the next fifteen years. So initially the Ricardo's are right to aspire to a goal of $1,000,000 in long-term savings, within a fifteen year timeframe, however they are also sensible to simply plan on achieving $300,000 for now. There is no point in aiming towards a goal of $1,000,000 at this stage because they just don't believe it is possible.

Now that's not to say that it's not possible, it's just that they don't see how it is possible right now. So while saving $1,000,000 is still their goal, it is still their aspiration, on a practical level they are happy enough to focus on achieving $300,000 within that time frame, as a bare minimum.

This goes against the popular beliefs which are put forward, by so many self-help gurus, who suggest that we should aim to achieve a goal and not worry about how realistic it is, rather than through our sheer belief, the universe will be forced to manifest this reality. What I am proposing here sounds like sheer blasphemy, to all those who aspire to the law of attraction. However, to clarify this subject, I am not against the law of attraction, however, certainly we cannot achieve anything unless we believe in it, and it is belief which is more important than aspiration!

The law of attraction can only work, if you really belief in the goal which has been set. So if you have doubts about your ability to achieve a certain goal, then it will not be achieved. From my perspective, I recommend that you aspire to any goal that you wish for, however, when it comes to planning, plan for a goal which you believe in, even if this goal is a far smaller goal.

For example, with the Ricardo's, they aspire for a $1,000,000, however, they don't have any believable way, at this point in time to plan to achieve this. Now for some individuals this will work out just fine. They have an iron clad believe in their goal, they just know it can be achieved.

If this is the case with you, then great, just gun yourself towards actualizing that goal. However, on the other hand, if you are like the vast majority of human beings, doubts will exist, and the doubts are perfectly natural. Because most of us have underachieved most of the time, we find it difficult to reconcile our aspirations with our beliefs!

I don't care how many self-help books you read, or to what degree you buy into the highly popular concept of the law of attraction, unless your belief in the goals which have been made are ironclad, they will not be achieved, simply because of the doubts which will arise, which still fulfils the law of attraction, but in a negative manner, because your negative beliefs are getting in the way!

In this way, it is very much a catch 22 situation, whereby we aspire to something, however, unless we have already achieved that state, it becomes next to impossible to achieve this goal!

Basically human beings are incapable of achieving something which is far beyond their experiential range!

So how to get past this catch 22 scenario?

The simplest way to do this is by aspiring to the big goal, but planning towards the fulfilment of a smaller, more believable goal. It is interesting that we readily accept the achievement of small initial and intermediate goals, in certain areas such as academics and vocational achievement, for example. However, when we think in terms of personal life achievement; there is a general tendency towards shooting for the stars.

Take a medical student for example, in most Countries medical studies last approximately five years, followed by a year of internship. Now the goal of becoming a doctor, of being able to possess a thorough understanding of the human body, the human anatomy, physiology, the various diseases and their cures; the ability to diagnose and cure a plethora of conditions; to be able to deliver a baby and to conduct minor surgical procedures; all of these represent the minimum amount of know-how, which a doctor requires, in order to receive their degree and their medical registration. This is without pursuing graduate studies or specialization, just the stuff of your regular doctor, fresh out of medical school!

It's a challenging proposition to learn so much, and in a relatively small period of time. However do you think that the medical schools of the World set the goal of achieving all of this at the outset of the course?

Well no! Rather year one and two tends to be focused on learning non-clinical subjects. Then they move onto clinical subjects, and then into actual practice, within a hospital environment. Regarding exams, there are a plethora of exams, which need to be passed, and would be doctors have several goals to aspire to. Firstly, passing the non-clinical subjects final exam, then passing the clinical subject final exam and then successfully completing the internship exam.

So we see, in the example of the comprehensive training which is required to become a doctor, that the medical training authorities reduce the difficult goal of medical training, down to three major goals and then each of these three goals are subsequently reduced down to a series of smaller goals, which are the individual subject exams. Subsequently, would be doctors while aspiring to medical greatness, actually plan to pass the various exam stages, one stage at a time, otherwise the goal would be totally untenable.

This is exactly where so many self-help programs go wrong, by emphasizing the completion of a great sounding goal, but one which is ultimately neither believable nor doable for most program participants!

While the law of attraction works, it can only work as long as you are capable of achieving the goal. The best way to achieve a goal which appears to be outside of your comfort zone is to reduce it down into a series of smaller goals which are believable!

We have seen the example of the Ricardo's who are aspiring to a goal of saving $1,000,000 in fifteen years, however they are planning on saving at least $300,000, because they see that as believable.

In real World terms, as their income increases, they will simply add to the savings fund, and over time they will reset the finical goal to $500,000 then $750,000 and then finally $1,000, 000. We can see that at the outset they only begin to put money into long-term savings, after they have cleared of their debts and taken a family holiday, which is about two and a half years into the wealth creation process, and even at this stage they are only saving $437 a month!

However, by the end of the fourth year they are saving anywhere between $937 and $1437 per month. At that rate of the increase in their savings, we can imagine how much money they will be saving per month by the end of year 10!

The points which I am rising here are abstruse ones, which is why I am taking pains to elaborate upon them. But in a nutshell, the essence of the five keys program is to aspire to achieve the Sun, Moon and stars, however, on a practical level the emphasis is to achieve greatness one step at a time, and incrementally progress towards big goals over a period of years.

While it may sound conservative, it's the sort of thinking which will help the majority of individuals achieve what they want to achieve, whereas society tends to idealize individuals who make great achievements very quickly. However, at any one time only a small number of people can manage to achieve great results, in a small period of time!

If you are talented enough, or fortunate, enough to achieve greatness within a short turnaround time, then this is great, however from a tactical point of view the 5 pillars program has to presume that most participants are ordinary people, who have ordinary abilities and only the average quantum of good look on their side. While it's great to celebrate big achievements, in others, surely a really effective self-help system should be able to make the most humble participant achieve good results over time, and this is what we are setting out to achieve in the 5 pillars. By improving, year by year, and leveraging one success on top of another until we achieve the goals which we really want to achieve.

Fortunately, most of us don't want to be the next astronaut to fly to the Moon, or the next Mark Zukerberg. These kinds of goals are particularly difficult to achieve, because at any one time there are only a handful of astronauts walking the planet and an even smaller number of billionaires!

However to aspire to becoming a millionaire, to financial freedom, to owning a nice house, a nice car or cars and to travelling the World, basically these are the ordinary desires which excite most of us, and are really quite achievable. However, they might take time to achieve, and unless you can generate a lot of money quickly the only way to have these nice achievements and possessions, is by leveraging financial success over a period of years, and selecting goals which are achievable and believable in your eyes!

We can all attend a weekend program, whereby we learn some new things about ourselves and where we get boosted by our participation. However, when we return back to work on Monday morning, all too quickly reality slips back in. It's like the holiday high were we travel to some tropical destination, for a week, where we eat and drink like a king and for a little while our World vision broadens, only to shrink back just as quickly within a week or two of returning home!

On the face of it, the slow pace of the 5 pillar program might sound unexciting, as to say the focus on planning to have small goals, however, over a period of years the results keep increasing exponentially and this is where true success lies!

So say for example, you want to save $1,000,000 in 10 years, and at present you have $100,000 in debt and are paying out a $2,000 a month simply to service the minimum payments on your debts. Well the first thing, is to clear off the debt which will free up $2,000 a month, then do some prioritization, about how to spend the $2,000 a month, towards fulfilling goals, and put aside a certain amount of it towards long term financial wealth.

Where this differs from most self-help programs, is that most programs would suggest setting a goal of $1,000, 000 and dividing it by 10 to provide a yearly goal and then by 12 to provide a monthly goal. However, this breaks down to a goal of $8,333 a month, which is a lot!

Furthermore a couple of years down the road, if you check in on your progress and see that you should have amassed $200,000, when in fact you have only amassed $30,000, chances are you will become disillusioned!

The other error, which many self-programs give, is by providing no kind of short term goal at all. They suggest that you simply believe that $1,000, 000 will come from somewhere, mysteriously over the next ten years.

This is the same sort of mentality which has some people paying out a $100 a week on lottery tickets every week, whereby they cling onto the dream of success and believe that surely someday their boat will come in simply because of the small fortune which they have spent on lottery tickets. Sad to say $100 a week on lottery tickets accrues to $5,200 a year.

In reality, the statistical odds of winning a lottery are so remote that you might as well buy one lottery ticket every decade or so, because either your luck is in or its not, because there is absolutely no way to game the system, the only way to definitely win the lottery is by buying so many tickets that the lottery payout is actually less than the amount of money which you spent in order to win!

Just take a look at the graphs below, which compare the fallacy of the two most popular self-help wealth promotion ideologies. The first one, the 'law of attraction' is based upon belief that the money will come mysteriously out of somewhere, while the second one which is the fallacy of 'reverse engineering', is based on the assumption that you can make perfect linear progress towards all of your goals!

The Law of Attraction Fallacy!

The Reverse Engineering Fallacy!

Summary

Here are the central tenets of long term investment planning which will work both practically and motivationally!

Aspire to a great goal, and don't get too hung up over the practicality of the goal. For practical purposes set yourself goals, which are both believable and doable.

Because if you do not believe, in your ability to achieve a goal, or select a goal which is way beyond your present skills and circumstances, then more than likely your own lack of faith in yourself, will self-sabotage your efforts!

In order to motivate yourself, have a think about what you feel is believable and doable considering your present circumstances, and then work towards that goal.

Because you are now highly motivated, the doable goal begins not only to be achieved, but also to be exceeded. At this stage revise the doable goal upwards, and keep on doing this until you either achieve the original aspirational goal, or at least get as near to it as possible.

By following these steps, at the very least you will have the motivation necessary to achieve the doable goal, and chances are that some revisions will take place, so that you will quite possibly either fulfil the original goal, or at least come close to it. So maybe in the example above the $1,000, 000 may not be achieved, however perhaps $500,000 will be achieved instead, which is still pretty good!

By following this realistic approach, you will manage to gain form the aspirational aspects of the law of attraction, without becoming demotivated by a vague and unbelievable goal, which does not appear to be progressing. Also you will gain from the highly targeted approach which is advocated by some programs whereby you set goals. Goals help us to move forward, however it is important not to become too hung up by them or once again demotivation will come about.

Finally, by managing a flexible approach to financial savings, it allows for the possibility of ups and downs in your finances, so that the most important factor is to keep moving forward, and maintaining the general belief that as circumstances improve, over time, that the amount of money being invested into savings will increase along the way!

The interesting thing about setting and meeting small goals is that they really do radically change your belief system. This is why most self-help courses fail to deliver results. The courses set out to sell themselves, by advertising the mind blowing benefits which comes from following their systems. However, while their theory is often good, they tend to fail to be of any use, because of an over emphasis on hitting big goals quickly.

Promising the delegates of a self-help course, that by following this program, that they can change their lives practically overnight, is a great sales gimmick. This gimmick tends to be backed up by testimonies, however, what percentage of delegates undergo life transformational experiences?

This is questionable. We can all cherry pick the best results and present these people by way of validation of our system. But surely, if a self-help system is that good, then the majority should see radical life change, and this never happens!

Throughout this book, I have gone into considerable lengths to counter the promises which are put forward by so many self-help gurus. By doing this, it is not my intention to be negative, or condescending. However, I do feel that there is a truth which is being relegated here. Behind all the self-help promotional material, lies a business concept, whereby individuals are trained in how to become more successful.

In and of itself, this is a good thing. However, somewhere along the way, the majority of proponents of self-help systems, got carried away with their promises, so that it became something of a necessity to make all sorts of wild claims in order to fill up a self-help course. This is what I am against!

The majority of self-help theory is actually quite correct, however, the fact is that the majority of people do not progress. And this is because it is politically correct, only to make wild claims about what can beat achieved, by attending one of these courses. If a self-help guru where to suggest that the majority of delegates would gain very little by the course, I feel that they would have difficulty in selling seats to it!

However, if we really want our society to progress, and put an end to the endless struggling which is taking place in most peoples' lives, then shouldn't we be a little bit more honest about what can be really achieved?

Well I think so!

The emphasis behind the five keys, may well be a deeply conservative approach to life change, however, it is an honest one, and one which is quite doable, by the majority of ordinary people, who may well read this book.

You may also be wondering, why I am talking in so much detail about self-help courses and books, when the theme of this book is personal finance?

Well, the reason for this is simply because more than likely the reason for your present state of indebtedness is largely psychological in character. It is possible that you had some bad luck in your life; however, if you have had financial issues, for a long period of time, then chances are that attitudinal changes are required, on your part.

By and large, this book has focused upon explaining the flaws in the present educational system, and how it is essential to upgrade ones financial World view, in order to become debt free, and to move on towards a wealthier and more fulfilling life.

However, there is also a need to challenge oneself, in relation to beliefs, ideals, and aspirations and so on. Simply put, if you know very little about yourself and your real motivations, then I would suggest that you start reading and working through some self-help material, because chances are that you have some negative beliefs, which are holding you back.

I strongly advise all readers of this book, to do some work on themselves, however, just keep in mind that there is a lot of material out there which will suggest that you can turn your life around simply by thinking so. However, action, and massive action at that is actually required to make this changes. Furthermore, while it is true that we attract things into our life, it must also be borne in mind that we are restricted, not so much by external events, but rather by our own beliefs!

Back in the 1950's and 60's positive thinking really took off. However most people found it did not work for them, and this is because while they thought positive, they did not belief positive. Their negative beliefs foiled their results. In this regards the law of attraction advocates a focus on belief rather than thinking, and in this way it is quite correct. However, most of us cannot change our beliefs, without changing our actions. Its biofeedback, we need to make some small wins in order to begin to believe in what we are doing, and this is where the law of attraction falls down!

Action, action and more action, is the mantra which we have to follow. Amend a behaviour, deliver small results, rinse and repeat that's the way to go!

Like I noted earlier, I'm not against self-development methodologies, and indeed I do advise all readers of this book to do some self-development work on themselves. But do beware, that most of what is promised out there simply doesn't work, because it denies the reality of the power of human action and the necessity to undergo belief change via positive experiential feedback!

Belief is a funny thing, whatever way you look at it there is no success like success! Even a small success inspires a bigger goal next time and so on!

So remember, with financial planning, realistic goal setting means goals which you can believe in and over time you can skip hop and jump to bigger and better financial goals over time!

Finally, do remember that this pillar is about long-term goals. I know that thinking in terms of 10 years sounds really too far away, but this is just the kind of thinking which the wealthy possess, and it is necessary to get your head around this concept, if want to achieve long term wealth!

Second step in financial planning

Deciding upon an investment vehicle

This is the most difficult aspect of financial planning, because the World of financial investment is a complicated and volatile environment to operate in. As a rule of thumb, most generic investment vehicles, provided by your local bank or brokerage service will probably provide you with an investment plan which will be fairly inflexible and which will just about cover inflation, if you are lucky. So while this is better than leaving your money in a bag under your mattress, it's still not all that great.

On the other extreme, you can go for all sorts of high risk investments, such as some of the riskier financial products which are available on the stock market, such as calls and puts for instance. However, while these investments may produce amazing returns, often they are extremely high risk and will often produce terrible losses in the long-term.

So briefly put, it's all about leverage; the greater the leverage the greater potential both for gains and losses.

In a bull market, often the riskier investment vehicle will produce the greatest levels of returns without too much risk. However once the bull run ends, the sudden market turndown ends up wiping out most of the investors in these markets. So unless you really know your stuff, chances are that you will end up, sooner or later, getting wiped out by these risky investments!

Then again, you can go into the midrange financial products, such as mutual funds or hedge funds. Often they produce good returns over time, although as a downside your money tends to be locked in and often these funds lose money much of the time, although over the long term they usually make good returns. Of course, at the moment, the World stock market is demonstrating great volatility, so there really is no fund which is really safe at the moment!

Other options include foreign currency investing and even gold, silver and other rare mineral investments. Great gains can be made here, and also lost. Once again it's pretty high risk, unless you really know what you are doing!

Bonds are also potential money makers, but then again most bonds are locked in for a very long period of time, and really the World economy is so volatile these days that you would want great faith to trust in any investment plan whereby your money is locked in for 10 years!

Finally, although quite unpopular at the moment, real estate investment is another potential investment vehicle. While real estate has developed a bad reputation, since the global downturn, it must be remembered that someone is always making on real estate, and the reason why most real estate investors got burnt in 2008-2009 is because they overstretched themselves!

At the moment many properties are under-priced, and really if you can afford to buy a property and sit on it, it will nearly always make money in the long term, especially if it is able to cash flow itself via renting, for instance. The vital thing to understand with real estate investing is that it really is a long term investment. While great money can be earned by flipping properties, for a quick profit in a bull market, when the market goes from bull to bear you may end up sitting on properties, in some case for a decade or longer!

If this concept scares you then veer away from real estate investing!

Deciding Upon an Investment Vehicle

which Fits in with Your Financial Planning

Deciding upon an investment vehicle is not an easy thing to arrive at because of the enormous range and variation in risk factors, with risk versus return varying from no risk and no worthwhile return right across to great return but terrible risk!

My advice to you, when carrying out financial planning, is to really take account of your personal circumstances and skillsets and then carry out lots of research. Remember if you go to a financial planning broker, without having a thorough understanding of the potential financial products which they are offering, is akin to a sheep heading into the shearing parlour!

Now while you may find it abhorrent to think that some sales people will ignore your long term good simply so they can make a commission, but there you go, it's a dog eat dog World out there, and the last thing you want is to finish paying off debt only to blow your new found savings on a bad investment product!

So what to do about it?

As noted, there really is no generic answer for you, rather it is necessary to do some Soul searching and also have a look at your skillsets. For example, if you are interested in stocks and shares, it will not work well for you unless you are willing to check up with it every day, and you are happy carrying out some analytics on the figures. Also with real estate, it's all about persistence and passion, so unless you like it do not get into it!

Another possibility to go for is a diverse product range. Although personally I would sooner pick my own range of diversified financial portfolio, rather than trusting it to some mutual fund manager who is only doing his/her job, simply because no one cares more about my investments than me!

My final word of advice is to go down the conservative route rather than the risky route. After all the aim of long term investment is to make a bundle of money over a 15 to 20 year timeframe. Try to avoid putting all your eggs in one basket, and keep away from get rich quick schemes. To put a perspective, on risky financial planning, say you were in debt for 5 years, and then after paying off debt, you invested your new found savings over 15 years, only to lose everything in year 15 due to some risky investments, how would that make you feel?

So play it safe and slow, and you will get there in the end, and once you achieve a small goal, move on up to a bigger goal and so on!

And do remember that the wealthy become wealthy not just because of income, or because they invest for the long term, but also because they are willing to learn how to make money, they get passionate about it! If you want to get good at anything, you have to get passionate about it. So don't just buy into to some slick salesman sales pitch or buy into some waffle you have hear from a friend of a friend at your local bar!

Do your research and be willing to slowly roll out your financial plan!

Chapter Seven – Putting the Five Keys to Debt Freedom Together

Hopefully you have enjoyed reading your way through the 5 keys.

The central point, behind the 5 pillars, is that being indebted is simply a series of bad financial habits, which come about as a result of poor financial beliefs which came about because of some degree of denial. All of which result in you making purchases on your credit cards, as well as other lines of credit, in an effort to ease the inner tension. While this is terrible, the same processes which got you into debt can get you out of debt too!

You can get out of debt by following these simple tactics:

- Stop accruing debt on your credit cards

- Learn to budget

- Put some money aside so as to protect the debt reduction process

- Creating and following short to medium term goals so as to both reduce debt and keep yourself debt free, once you finish paying off debt

- Creating a long-term wealth production plan via intelligent financial planning

Simply by following these steps, it is possible to stop accruing debt, to finish paying off debt, to remain debt free and even to become wealthy over the medium to long-term!

The big fantasy, behind credit card debt and indeed all debt is that debt is situational, that it is simply some bad luck which has come your way! However, if this were really true then why are some people in lots of debt, regardless of their income, while other people are well off, even if they are on small income?

This leads onto another debt reduction myth, which is that people with a big income have no debt, while people on a small income are always in debt!

In reality, many indebted people are in debt regardless of income, while some people on a small income are in fact debt free and even quite wealthy in some cases. While it is difficult to remain debt free, if your income is very low, in reality for most debtors they are indebted because of their poor financial beliefs and habits. While it will take someone on a small income a longer time to become wealthy, in realty most people are capable of either becoming indebted or wealthy; it's really a matter of choice!

While this may sound like a ridiculous concept, it is the truth, we select whether or not we are poor or wealthy!

As long as we are not taking responsibility, for our actions and drifting in our lives, it is a given that sooner or later we will end up in a state of indebtedness, because that's simply the way of the World in which we live in. If you want to live an abundant wealthy life, then you have to start by taking responsibility for your actions, and get going with paying off debt. Then once the debt is clear, simply use intelligent financial planning to create wealth, and get your head around the reality, that most of us can only become wealthy over the long term rather than the short term!

While the voyage through the 5 pillars is a little bit mysterious and daunting, the one really good thing to take from all of this, is that whatever your financial reality, it is a product of your thoughts and feelings and that regardless of your level of credit card debt, auto debt, home loan debt etc., you can become debt free!

Many debtors are paying off debt and becoming debt free on a daily basis, so why not you? And if you are focused enough, even on a small income, you can, via intelligent financial planning, become wealthy in the long term!

So don't become daunted by the prospect, review the various steps, in the five pillar program, and do some financial planning, and regardless how long it takes, get going with transforming your finances, and get going today!

Finally on the subject of time and action, in order to read this book you have taken out time, your viable time to do so.

While it is a good thing to read informative books, it is an even greater thing to apply the suggestions, which have been made in this and other good books! I know that much of the material which has been presented is slightly technical in nature and also that many of the concepts are slightly beyond the normal way of thinking about personal finance, and that new ideas take a little time to digest and to make sense of. If you have enjoyed this book, and the concepts which have been presented, then do take out the time to assimilate the ideas which have been presented and do undertake the exercises which have been presented.

Most Importantly, Action is Vital!

It may feel awkward to maintain a budgeting log and to carry out long term financial planning, however, if you cannot plan your finances, then someone else will do the planning for you, namely the advertising people who advertise all those great products which you would like to buy, but which you cannot presently afford! If you do not plan, then you are forced to follow the crowd and as we have seen in the recent economic turndown, the crowd has had their fingers badly burnt!

There are many presumptions, which we can fall into, and it can be ok to presume certain things, for example, I can presume that there will be food on the shelves of my local supermarket tomorrow, and lo and behold food will be there! I can presume that the buses and bin Lorries will work in my local town or City and yes they do! In our modern complex civilization we have to presume many things, because quite simply everything is so specialized that we simply have to presume that things will keep on working!

However, when it comes to such areas as personal finances, it is really up to us to take an active role. Perhaps twenty or thirty years ago it was possible to invest in a pension fund and presume that everything will be ok, however, in today's dynamic (and somewhat unpredictable) World economy, we simple have to take matters of personal finance in hand and take responsibility for our own finances!

Integrate the workbooks (which are at the end of this eBook). If you can't, then try to make amended versions of them which suit your particular personality and circumstances. Obviously some people need more detail and some people less, but I really ardently hope that the principals, which are presented in this volume, will take root in you and that you apply them in whatever mode works for you.

After all it's only through actions that you can change your life, and the essence of the 'five keys to credit card debt freedom' program is to help you to become free from debt, and in particular from credit card debts, which are the most intractable debts of all, due to their high interest rates!

Furthermore, the tendency to slip back into debt is always ever present, and the best way to guarantee that you dot slip back into debt, is simply to leverage your resources towards the acquisition of wealth, rather than to flitter them away on comfort spending!

You have the ability, not only to become debt free, but also to become wealthy, simply begin with small goals and as time progresses and positive results begin to come your way, great changes will take place in your life.

So get going and take some massive action today!

Thank You

Thank you for taking the time out of your busy schedule, if you have a chance please leave me a review, I'd appreciate that!

REVIEWS

PLEASE FEEL FREE TO POST A REVIEW. YOU CAN ACCESS MY AUTHORS PROFILE BY GOING TO WWW.AMAZON.COM THEN SELECTING BOOKS AND TYPING IN (DERMOT FARRELL – AUTHOR). THIS WILL BRING UP MY AUTHORS RPOFILE PAGE. YOU CAN THEN SELECT THIS BOOK AND WRITE A REVIEW, ALSO MY OTHER BOOKS ARE LISTED THERE

Footnotes

Chapter One - You Are Not Alone

The data in this chapter comes from several sources; the revolving debt per household figures from 1980 and 2010 come from "Bankruptcy Reform and Credit Cards" by Michelle J. White, a working paper number 13265, from the National Bureau of Economic Research, July 2007.

The figures for 2010 are courtesy of The Federal Reserve, Consumer Credit G.19 document, which can be found at the following link:

http://www.federalreserve.gov/releases/g19/HIST/cc_hist_sa.html

The revolving credit figure for March 31st 2010 was $84,2563.18. If we divide this by the number of households in the USA as per the US 2010 Census, the household figure is 116,716,292. So this brings an average household revolving debt figure for 2010 of $7,219. Also please do note that strictly speaking revolving credit also includes all forms of open ended credit, so not just credit cards, it also includes store cards, and home equity lines would also be considered as revolving credit. However, since credit cards account for 90% plus of the revolving credit figure, it is fair to say that revolving credit statistics present a fair figure of the state of credit card usage in the USA at any particular time!

The disposable income figures come from the Census website, www.census.gov. The document is the Table 679. "Selected Per Capita Income and Product Measures in Current and Chained (2005) Dollars". This table can be found on the www.census.gov website under the table reference 12s0679.

Footnote 1:

Revolving debts are debts which are without fixed terms. Although it includes such things as store cards and home credit lines, about 98% of it is made up of credit card debt.

Footnote 2:

The Census Abstract for 2012 outlines both the projected debt figures, as well as the average number of credit card holders. The figure of a projected debt figure of 2012 of $870,000,000,000, divided by 160 million Americans possessing credit cards, suggest an average outstanding credit card debt of $5,437 per credit card holder.

These projections also appear to be verified by the Federal Reserve table (http://www.federalreserve.gov/releases/g19/HIST/cc_hist_sa.html) which outlines the various debts across the nation on a quarterly basis. Just take a look at the middle column figure for March 2012 and it reads $803,634.37. Now multiply this figure by 1,000,000 (as the table lists debts in multiples of millions of dollars), and the figure becomes $803,634,370,000, then divide it by 160,000,000 credit card holders and the average debt figure becomes $5,022.71 average credit card debt per credit card holder!

In reality everyone's outstanding credit card debt will vary, however, the statistics reveal a widespread tendency towards retaining an outstanding debt in the thousands of dollars on a yearly basis. Considering that this debt is undergoing double digit interest rate, that's a lot of unnecessary debt which a great many people are accruing, simply because they are retaining debt on their credit cards, over a long period of time!

Footnote 3 - Moody's April 2012 report on credit card delinquency rates:

Moody's is one of America's biggest credit rating agencies. They produce reports throughout the year on a wide variety of financial statistics and credit ratings, not only for America but also for every Country around the World. To find out more about the statistical information which they have on offer you can visit their website, which is http://www.moodys.com/.

Footnote 4 - A note on stakeholders:

We mention stakeholders here, because each decision maker is a stakeholder. In the case of a husband and wife, with young kids, there are two stakeholders. However, in some families, other members will also be stakeholders. We see in this sometimes in extended families, whereby perhaps elderly parents are living with one or more of their children or grandchildren, and whereby their resources are pooled together.

As a rule of thumb, whenever resources are pooled together for the long-term, then all people involved should be stakeholders in the decision making process.

The issue of stakeholders will vary from household to household. For example, in one household an adult child, maybe staying with their parents, however, their finances are completely separate from each other, in which case if the parents wish to do some budgeting then they do not have to consider the adult child as being a stakeholder. However, in another family, the adult child is clearly staying with their parents for the long-term and their finances are inextricably linked, In this case the child will have to be considered as a stakeholder.

However, another example from the opposite perspective is that of an elderly parent, who is under the care of their children and whose finances are the responsibility of their adult child. However, the elderly parent may be old and disabled and possibly mentally incompetent. In this case, while the adult child has to consider the wellbeing of their parent, they are hardly likely to consider their parent as a stakeholder, since they are presently incapable of any decision making!

Chart Two – Median Value of Debt for Families with Holdings

The data for this graph comes from "2007 Survey of Consumer Finances Chart book", p 831. The precise data on this graph is listed below. Please bear in mind that all figures have been chained to year 2007 figures, so when we compare 1989 debts at an average of $24,100 to 2007 average debts of $67,300, we are comparing figures in 1997 dollars! So the jump from 1989 average household debt to 2007 average household debt is 179%!

Appendix

Free Financial Worksheets

Monthly Expenditure Worksheet

Date	Expenditure Type	$	Date	Expenditure Type	$

Expense Totals				**Expense Totals**			
				Month Expenses			

Family Buffer Account

Month	Comment	Credit	Debit	Balance
January				
February				
March				
April				
May				
June				
July				
August				
September				
October				
November				
December				

Blue Sky Thinking Financial Planning – Date:

	Long Term Ideal Goals – Person One	Long Term Ideal Goals – Person Two
1		
2		
3		
4		
5		
6		
7		
8		
9		

10		
11		
12		

Financial Planning – Silly Wish Reduction Exercise

Date:

	Wish	Not Now	Doable
1			
2			
3			
4			
5			
6			
7			
8			
9			

10			
11			
12			

Prioritization list – Date

Time Frame	Person One	Person Two	Priority List	Priority#

Time Frame	Person One	Person Two	Priority List	Priority#

Summary of Goals – Date:

Goals	Priority	Timeframe	Short/Medium/Long-Term

Goal Monitoring Worksheet – Date:

Month	Date	Credit Card Payment	Overdraft Facility	Loans
1				
2				
3				
4				
5				
6				
7				
8				
9				
10				
11				
12				
13				
14				
15				
16				
17				

18				
19				
20				
21				
22				
23				
24				

www.ingramcontent.com/pod-product-compliance
Lightning Source LLC
Chambersburg PA
CBHW071421180526
45170CB00001B/180